Changing Light

The Eternal Cycle of Night and Day

edited and with
artwork by

J. Ruth Gendler

HarperCollins*Publishers*

The art by J. Ruth Gendler that appears in this book
includes batiks, collages, drawings and mixed media pieces.
Changing Light was designed and produced by Marian O'Brien.
Permission acknowledgments appear on page 133 and following.

FIRST EDITION

Library of Congress Cataloging-in-Publication Data

Gendler, J. Ruth (Janet Ruth)
     Changing light : the eternal cycle of night and day /
  J. Ruth Gendler. — 1st ed.
       p.   cm.
     Includes bibliographical references.
     ISBN 0-06-092447-0
     1. Life—Literary collections. 2. Night—Literary
     collections. 3. Moon—Literary collections. I. Title.
PN6071.L6G46 1991
808.8'0345—dc20   90-56344

94 95 RRD 10 9 8 7 6 5 4 3 2

CONTENTS

SUNSET INTO EVENING

> The orphan boat of my heart
> Crosses the unsteady, undulant
> Ocean of Time.
> > *Ping Hsin*

NIGHT

> Where will you and I sleep?
> At the down-turned jagged rim of the sky,
> you and I will sleep.
> > *Wintu tribe "Dream Song"*

WITH THE DAWNING LIGHT

You wake from dreams of doom and—for a moment—
you know: beyond all the noise and the gestures,
the only real thing, love's calm unwavering flame
in the half-light of an early dawn.

Dag Hammarskjold

DAY

The moon and sun are travelers through eternity.
Even the years wander on. Whether drifting through
life on a boat or climbing toward old age leading a horse,
each day is a journey, and the journey itself is home.

Basho

TWILIGHT (DARK AND LIGHT TOGETHER)

> *"It was true during the night and it was
> true during the day."*
>
> *Wings of Desire*

INTRODUCTION

For thousands of years our ancestors marked the daily cycle of dark and light with poems, prayers, stories, songs. Recognizing the repetition and variation of changing light was a matter of survival as well as sacred knowledge. Throughout the world people have prayed at the border between sleep and waking, turned their faces east to greet the sun, chanted and taken purifying baths at dawn, offered sun salutations in the morning and sun dances on special days, petitioned the moon with love poems, counted their month from new moon to new moon. Children's lullabies were often a kind of prayer for singing the child to a safe sleep.

The traditional Catholic prayer cycle includes prayers for the eight canonical hours. Traditional Moslems pray five times a day; Jews gather in groups of ten for morning, late afternoon, and evening prayers. In medieval Europe *The Book of Hours* presented a series of prayers, psalms, stories from the lives of Jesus and Mary in words and pictures. It was the main book in people's homes, a beautifully illustrated manuscript arranged according to the church hours: matins, lauds, prime, terce, sext, nones, vespers, complines.

Time Sanctified is the title of a contemporary book about the Book of Hours. This title is startling to our modern ears; sacred time is not a part of our lives. At the doorway of the 21st century in our rush to be on time and take time off most of us don't give much attention to how we live in time. Feeling controlled by time, we in turn try to control and conquer time. At night we watch the stars on television instead of the stars in the sky.

Both the Trappist monk Thomas Merton and the Jewish scholar Abraham Heschel wrote movingly about sacred time. *Merton was convinced that if you let the hours of the day saturate you, and you gave them time, something would happen. He said that one of the best things that happened to him when he became a hermit was "being* attentive to the times of the day: when the birds begin to sing, and the deer came out of the morning fog, and the sun came up…. The whole thing boils down to giving ourselves in prayer a chance to realize that we have what we seek. We don't have to rush after it. It was there all the time, and if we give it time, it will make itself known to us…. There is in all this a sense of the unfolding of mystery in time, a reverence for gradual growth."[1]

Abraham Heschel described sacred time in contrast to sacred space. Heschel wrote, "The higher goal of spiritual living is not to amass a wealth of information, but to face sacred moments…. Spiritual life begins to decay when we fail to sense the grandeur of what is eternal in time…. Jewish ritual may be characterized as the art of significant forms in time, an architecture of time. Most of its observances… depend on a certain hour of the day or season of the year."[2]

My own attention to time and light is both recent and long-standing. As this anthology of night and day grew, I found myself spending time in the children's sections of libraries as well as immersed in prayerbooks, poems, anthropology texts. It seems that children, poets and lovers, farmers, and people in daily prayer are the ones who stay most alive to day changing into night changing into day. Every day and every night is a different experience of time and light, yet day and night are a constant pair.

The daughter of a clock collector, I must have learned a long time ago that we can measure time in numbers—seconds, minutes, hours, months, years, decades—or we can measure time by light—sunset, morning, late afternoon, twilight, evening.

When I began teaching as a California Poet in the Schools, one of the first poems I brought to elementary and junior high students was called "Learning to Tell Time" by an Iowa poet named Mary Jo Homstad. The poem travels through the hours of the day associating them with animals, with activities, with landscapes. Homstad begins: Eight a.m. "It is the hour of the *dreamstealers, the hour/of the fish, the hour that is hooked and brought/ flopping into the day."* Ten a.m. is *"the hour with an eye/it is the hour of the prairie... it is the hour that has all the maps."* Four p.m. is *"the hour that saves string."*[3]

     Schoolchildren who watch the wall clock through the hours of the school day write about hours easily; adults who long ago gave up any thought of writing "poetically" also could borrow this form and infuse it with their own sense of time.

     I began to ask students if they were "morning people or night people" and read a few more poems that touched on night and darkness, including Louise Bogan's poem "Night" and D. Patrick Miller's "Early Darkness." When Miller showed me the poem "Early Darkness," he wondered aloud about the image of washing the bowl and overturning it for night. As a batik artist who had dyed cloth and kept it in the bowl a long time waiting for the indigo dye to set, I loved these images. The dark ink we use in the day is somehow of the same stuff as the night sky.

     Somewhere in this time period, I bought a sketchbook of black paper and began pushing the paper to its limit, with oil pastel and gouache. Drawing on black paper fascinated me. With white paper, it is possible not to see the paper at all, to treat it as a blank surface to which we busily add our marks, filling it in, covering up the whole page. The black page is an undeniable presence; I couldn't pretend I was starting with nothing, I was working with black. And just as dancers have appeared in my artwork before I knew how much I love to move, so night and the hills at night were in my art before they were in my life.

     Are you a morning person or a night person? So often the students, little guys, eight, nine, ten, would claim night, would write about two a.m., three a.m., the hours when there were no authorities to answer to, no sibling to fight with. I, on the other hand, identified myself as a morning person. In friendship with night people, I often stayed up late, feeling the next day as if I had stolen time from my work, wondering why is it easier to do difficult tasks at nine in the morning than at two in the afternoon or 7:30 p.m.? I feel almost like a different person at different times of day, in different kinds of light. I found myself wishing for a week with eight mornings, four afternoons, six evenings. A month of mornings.

Often as I work, I follow the light around the house from writing in the morning at the desk with a window facing the eastern light to the drawing table in the studio which faces west to San Francisco Bay—in the late afternoon the sycamore trees seem to move inside the room to dance their leafy sunset dance across white walls. What shade is the shadow of green leaf and branch in July, of grey branch in late January?

A friend tells me that at certain difficult times she asks herself what makes her happy. At the top of the list she consistently writes light and shadow. What makes me happy? Being in the mountains at night and seeing the stars, sunlight in a forest, waking up in a room with eastern light without an alarm clock right before dawn, seeing the sun set and the moon rise at the same time, walking in the hills at sunset, trees at dusk, houses at night.

Astronomers discuss light and shadow effects; architects measure luminance and illuminance, religious texts from the *Rg Veda* to the *Zohar* to *The Egyptian Book of the Dead* are suffused with images of luminosity and radiance. Light spills over, light breaks through, light drenches us as thoroughly as rain. I listen eagerly as perceptive artists talk about kinds of light. Drawing with lines of light. Light bites into things. Light hits the Pacific and strikes off the ocean waters. Walking in the redwood fog, everything is lit from within. Over my desk three words: "Light determines form." We are all described by light. Defined by light. Outlined by light.

A few summers ago I began walking with a friend at night, and discovered the joy of walking at the end of the day. From the hills the city lights mirror the star lights, no less beautiful, even if we mourn the way they take away from the true blackness of the night sky.

Women in our culture have had much to fear from the night. Afraid of night, afraid to walk, we stay inside our houses and apartments because we've been told since childhood it's not safe. During those night walks I began to fall in love with night, almost as if night were a place, with the qualities of place, not time, a place one could visit again and again. As the 12th century Afghani poet Rumi says *"Night goes back to where it was./Everyone returns home sometime./Night, when you get there,/tell them how I love you."*[4] In her piece on the desert Justine Toms is surprised to learn that night is there all the time; day comes and goes.

Women have been taught to be afraid of night. Yet night is often associated with us and assigned to us. Looking up the word *night* in a mythological dictionary, the definitions inform me that night is first evil, then female. I think of the immensely beautiful photographs of the blue-green, jewel-like earth seen in the vast dark space, of scientists who are investigating dark matter. I think how in recent times women have marched to "Take back the night."

As much as I simply wanted to collect poems and stories about night and day, I found myself needing to look at our associations with light and dark, how much Western culture fears darkness, otherness, night, depth and death. Night and day, sun and moon, dark and light. Twos, in balance, each half needing the other to complete itself, how often we make one good, one bad. We love the night, and yet we fear darkness. We long for the warmth of light but shrink from the naked clarity that accompanies it.

The dictionary defines *night* in terms of day and *day* in terms of night. Can we find a way to talk about light and dark without talking about good and bad? To love both day and night? Can we hold the beauty of both in the same breath?

As a child who liked families of rhymes and collected homonyms, I was always fascinated that the words *night* and *light* rhymed with each other and with the word *bright*. Opposites linked in sound. Brilliance, a quality of intelligence, is also a quality of light. The adjective *light* is the opposite of *dark*, but it also plays against the word *heavy*. We dismiss someone as a lightweight or give profundity weight—"that's heavy." *Light*, flimsy or easy, also means enlightened.

As I understand Eastern thought, notions of light and enlightenment are balanced by a deep respect for the yin, the feminine, the nourishing dark. Each contains the other, and we need both to grow. Lines from the Scandinavian poet Reide Eknar clarify the "both at once" of light and dark.

> In the seed, the genes whisper: stretch out for the light
>   and seek the dark
> And the tree seeks the light, it stretches out for the dark
> And the more darkness it finds, the more light it discovers.[5]

Or as the "Hymn to Ra" from *The Egyptian Book of the Dead* says: "*The truth of what we call our knowing is both light and dark. Men are always dying and waking. The rhythm between we call life.... I walk in the dark feeling darkness on my skin. Dawn always begins in the bones.*"[6]

The Book of Genesis begins with God creating light. What a contrast to discover South American and African creation stories where it is light all the time, and people need the dark to rest. In one South American story from the Tupi Indians of the

Amazon in Brazil it is the Great Snake's daughter who is ill and needs sleep because her eyes are dazzled by the sun. Her Indian husband sends his three most trusted servants in their canoe to the Great Snake to bring back night. The Great Snake places night in a hollow palm nut sealed with resin instructing the men that no one but the Great Snake's daughter open it. Of course, as strange sounds emerge from the palm nut the men ignore their instructions and let night out. In a story from the Kono people of Sierra Leone God gives the Bat a basket of darkness to carry to the moon. To my surprise I also found references in esoteric Judaism to a lamp of darkness.

Do we create ourselves out of our creation stories? Often the light or the night or the moon is stolen, the sun kicked into the sky. Who is the thief who brings light or lets darkness out of the bag? Among the Northwest Coast people it is Raven or Crow who steals the box that contains light and lets light loose upon the world. In *The Wishing Bone Cycle* the trickster is able to wish two and then three moons into the sky. An Australian story about the Sun woman who lives underground and her daughter who comes up to light our world every day and then returns at night to her mother has curious similarities to the story of Persephone and Demeter. In a Navaho story the laws are written in the stars, "printed in the sky where everyone can see them."

Western culture assumes night precedes day; we have also assumed the sun is male and moon is female. Yet there are sun goddesses and moon gods, dawn goddesses and night gods. The sun and moon appear as brother and sister, as husband and wife, as two brothers, two sisters. Occasionally a woman marries the sun.

Ancient peoples began their day at sunrise, noon, or sunset. Both traditional Jews and Moslems begin their day at sunset. The *Oxford English Dictionary* names: the *solar day*, which is reckoned from noon to noon: the *astronomical day*, reckoned from midnight to midnight; the *civil day*, from midnight to midnight; the *sidereal day*, the time between the successive meridianal transits of a star, or specifically of the first point of Aries, about four minutes shorter than the solar day. Time by light? Light years?

I feel as though pulling on this thread of night and day is unraveling a whole fabric. It's as if I picked up a key to a door, but when I open the door there's not a room on the other side of the door but a huge space, maybe a sky. I don't know where to look or what to look at first because everywhere I turn my eyes there is so much to see. I find myself wondering about ancient astronomy and calendars, the impact of the first clock towers built in medieval European villages, when watches became common, the relationship between the watches we wear on our wrist and the verb, *watch* as in look or observe, how our sense of night has been changed by the electric light bulb and 24-hour convenience stores, Indian goddesses of the dawn, Chinese and Egyptian night goddesses, the relationship between poetry and prayer.

I ask some students to draw a picture of time. Time as a line, time as a circle, Grandfather time, four trees in four seasons, the phases of the moon, the Hindu Goddess Kali. I imagine night and day as black and white rectangles, like pages, inside a bright spiral of time but time somehow remains both inside and outside a structure of dark and light.

Thinking about time makes me dizzy and leads me to the philosophy and physics aisles of the bookstore; considering night and day brings me to poetry. From an early age it seems I associated poetry with a kind of moon talk. An adolescent attempt at a poem began, "If I worship the moon, will you call me a poet?" The moon as muse, the one who infuses our sleeping and waking dreams with her strange magic.

I ask my grandfather who was born in the Ukraine at the beginning of this century about the moon, and he says, "Years ago we thought God was there on the moon. Now we know better. We used to have ceremonies on the new moon."

Trying to understand the relationship between poetry and prayer I read ancient hymns and prayers to the moon aloud, read Rumi aloud, read Whitman and Dickinson and Izumi Shikibu aloud. I read love poems, mostly set at night, in which we swim out past any shore we know. Reading love poems I hear so many kinds of love, so many kinds of light. Voices of inspiration in the night. We turn toward each other again and again to find love lighting up the night. Aloud I hear prayers as poetry of praise, aloud I hear how many poems become love songs to God.

Nowhere is this confusion clearer than in the poetry of Rumi. No one has written more generously or prolifically about love longing for God. Coleman Barks, the contemporary Rumi translator, circles around Rumi's pronouns and the constant blurring of identities. *In Rumi's poetry there is always the mystery of the pronouns. Who is this you he addresses? Shams? Saladin Zarkub? Husam? The inner, angelic counterpart? The divine Beloved? A God-Person alloyed of the longing of lover for Beloved? The Friend?... Pronouns dissolve within the pressure of Rumi's recognition of his true identity. The essential power of Rumi's poetry is ecstasy, an ecstasy melting the confinement of the ego in to a larger, elastic, cross-pollinating dance of Selves.... No pronoun can speak the reality he experiences. There must remain a splendid mystery in the presence/s of Rumi's poems. It is the secret recognition...of friend and Friend, Rumi and Shams, actual personality and divine being, coordinate identities between and among.... Rumi's odes and quatrains rather are the personal, human records of a man's being given a sharp, clear consciousness of the divine, and enduring it.*[7]

In our quest for easy answers, in a culture of marketing where *light* is lite and *luminescence* is a shampoo, most people don't listen to poetry. In our time we commonly view poetry as a rarified form that doesn't have much to do with our lives. Many of us stay away, afraid it will either be too abstract and inaccessible or sentimental and precious.

Yet, poetry may be the more precise language we have for talking about the world. Poets who give language to states where the soul meets the world; the inner and outer intersect are charged and changed by the energy at the edge. In the introduction to her *Collected Poems* Kathleen Raine writes: *No one can suppose that the English language is any longer in its prime; words are worn thin with trivial use, emptied of meanings unknown in our materialist society. We are beset through press and media with a daily flood of words put to mean uses. Yet the soul still needs a roof over her head other than the breeze-blocks and acrylic paint of the world deemed real by media in the service of consumerism.... My mother, as she peeled the potatoes, inhabited her world of Border ballads, Shelley's skies, Milton's hells. The material commonplace, currently celebrated as the 'real' reality, has never been so for poetry, unless illuminated by the soul's inner light.*[8]

When I was in the beginning stages of this project, an editor friend asked me how my anthology would be useful. What a question! First, I wanted to reject the question—why does everything have to be useful. I didn't know how to articulate that poetry and myth are food for me, as necessary as bread and water. Before I knew how this material might be considered useful, I knew how to use it. Read these pieces aloud, find the lines that make sense to you, read outside, take this book outside and sit and read. Let these images feed you, let the sounds of these words nourish you.

Poets and artists have long walked along the border of their cultures, with their antennae alert to what's in the air and underground, with their eyes open to the light and dark. Poetry, myth, prayer attempt to translate, to bring across into words, the soul's journey to wholeness. They do not offer easy answers but a language which travels and comes home, a speech of heart truth, ecstatic or sorrowful. This soul-language is a language of doors, a language of windows and mirrors, a language of light and dark, a language of fire and water, radiance and depth, a language that somehow (I'm never quite sure how) always includes silence.

After all my reading and research, it was on a trip to Death Valley that I truly began to sense and make sense of all these pieces as part of a whole. Not only the eternal and changing nature of night and day but of the human heart. So a piece from 9th century Spain or 10th century Japan is as contemporary as a current song, a psychology text. In Death Valley in the company of some very fine photographers I studied the sky. While they were photographing canyons and documenting stark layers of geological rock, I let myself hear how different voices in this book amplified and echoed and sung to each other until it became one long song we have been singing to each other through the centuries. Changing light. The eternal cycle of night and day.

J. Ruth Gendler
Spring 1991

NOTES

1. Brother David F.K. Steindl-Rast, "Recollections of Thomas Merton's Last Days in the West," quoted in *A Hidden Wholeness/ The Visual World of Thomas Merton*, photographs by Thomas Merton and John Howard Griffin, text by John Howard Griffin (Boston: Houghton Mifflin Company, 1979), p. 49.

2. Abraham Heschel, *The Earth Is the Lord's and The Sabbath* (New York: Harper & Row, 1966), pp. 6, 8.

3. Mary Jo Homstad, "Learning to Tell Time," *Weavings* (Denver: Bread & Butter Press, 1980) pp. 106-107.

4. Rumi, *Unseen Rain*, translated by John Moyne and Coleman Barks (Putney, VT: Threshold Books, 1986), p. 38.

5. Reide Eknar, from "Horologium," poem no. 11 (in Swedish) in *Mellan polerna* (Stockholm: Norstedts, 1982), or "Horologium," translated into English by the author.

6. "Hymn to Ra" in *Awakening Osiris: The Egyptian Book of the Dead*, translated by Normandi Ellis (Grand Rapids: Phanes Books, 1988), p. 218.

7. Rumi, *Open Secret,* translated by John Moyne and Coleman Barks (Putney, VT: Threshold Books, 1984), p. xi.

8. Kathleen Raine, *Selected Poems* (Great Barrington, MA: Lindisfarne Press, 1988), p. 5.

SUNSET

SUNSET

Slowly the west reaches for clothes of new colors
which it passes to a row of ancient trees.
You look, and soon these two worlds both leave you,
one part climbs toward heaven, one sinks to earth,

leaving you, not really belonging to either,
not so hopelessly dark as that house that is silent,
not so unswervingly given to the eternal as that thing
that turns to a star each night and climbs—

leaving you (it is impossible to untangle the threads)
your own life, time and standing high and growing,
so that, sometimes blocked in, sometimes reaching out,
one moment your life is a stone in you, and the next, a star.

RAINER MARIA RILKE
(1875-1926)
TRANSLATED FROM THE GERMAN BY ROBERT BLY

A land not mine, still
forever memorable,
the waters of its ocean
chill and fresh.

Sand on the bottom whiter than chalk,
and the air drunk, like wine,
late sun lays bare
the rosy limbs of the pinetrees.

Sunset in the ethereal waves:
I cannot tell if the day
is ending, or the world, or if
the secret of secrets is inside me again.

ANNA AKMATOVA
(1889-1966)
TRANSLATED FROM THE RUSSIAN BY JANE KENYON

The hair ornament of the sun
has sunk
into the legendary sea.

MITSUHASHI TAKAJO
(1899-1972)
TRANSLATED FROM THE JAPANESE BY
KENNETH REXROTH AND IKUKO ATSUMI

A PRAIRIE SUNSET

Shot gold, maroon and violet, dazzling silver, emerald fawn,
The earth's whole amplitude and Nature's multiform power
    consign'd for once to colors;
The light, the general air possess'd by them—colors till now
    unknown,
No limit, confine—not the Western sky alone—the high
    meridian—North, South, all,
Pure luminous color fighting the silent shadows to the last.

WALT WHITMAN
(1819-1892)

SERENE EVENING

A serene evening.
We spend it drinking wine.

The sun, going down,
lays its cheek against the earth
to rest.

The breeze lifts
the coattails of the hills.
The skin of the sky
is as smooth as the pelt
of the river.

How lucky we are to find
this spot for our sojourn
with doves cooing
for our greater delight.

Birds sing,
branches sigh
and darkness drinks up
the red wine of sunset.

MUHAMMAD IBN GHĀLIB AL RUSĀFI
(d. 1177)
TRANSLATED BY COLA FRANZEN
FROM THE SPANISH VERSIONS OF EMILIO GARCÍA GÓMEZ

PRAYING THE SUNSET PRAYER

I'll let you in on a secret
about how one should pray the sunset prayer.
It's a juicy bit of praying,
like strolling on grass,
nobody's chasing you, nobody hurries you.
You walk toward your Creator
with gifts in pure, empty hands.
The words are golden
their meaning is transparent,
it's as though you're saying them
for the first time.

If you don't catch on
that you should feel a little elevated,
you're not praying the sunset prayer.
The tune is sheer simplicity,
you're just lending a helping hand
to the sinking day.
It's a heavy responsibility.
You take a created day
and you slip it
into the archive of life,
where all our lived-out days are lying together.

The day is departing with a quiet kiss.
It lies open at your feet
while you stand saying the blessings.
You can't create anything yourself, but you
can lead the day to its end and see
clearly the smile of its going down.

See how whole it all is,
not diminished for a second,
how you age with the days
that keep dawning,
how you bring your lived-out day
as a gift to eternity.

JACOB GLATSTEIN
(1896-1971)
TRANSLATED FROM THE YIDDISH BY RUTH WHITMAN

EVENING PRAYER

Praised are You, Lord our God, King of the universe whose
word brings the evening dusk. You open the gates of dawn
with wisdom, change the day's divisions with understanding,
set the succession of seasons and arrange the stars in the sky
according to Your will. You create day and night, rolling
light away from darkness and darkness away from light.
Eternal God, Your rule shall embrace us forever. Praised are
You, Lord, for each evening's dusk.

FROM *SIDDUR SIM SHALOM*
TRANSLATED FROM THE HEBREW BY RABBI JULES HARLOW

WHAT THE ROSE SAID

I am the sea cut and folded.

I am the last evening
fallen on an enchanted shoulder.

MICHAEL HANNON
(1939-   )

Evening spreads across the sky.
Shadow that's still light
penetrates the light
that's already dust of shadow.
It's evening: the lost
color of evening,
the human face of evening,
the fatal sweetness of evening.

DIEGO VALERI
(1887-1976)
TRANSLATED FROM THE ITALIAN BY MICHAEL PALMA

Early Darkness

Think of it as ink:
an indigo dye descending
between the leaves of the trees
and down to the grasses.

There is no dying of the light—
just the washing of a bowl,
and overturning it for night.

When day arrives we must write with
    bottled darkness.
In the night we can dream
    free messages of light.

D. Patrick Miller
(1953-   )

If each day falls
inside each night,
there exists a well
where clarity is imprisoned.

We need to sit on the rim
of the well of darkness
and fish for fallen light
with patience.

Pablo Neruda
(1904-1973)
Translated from the Spanish by William O'Daly

9

NIGHT

KNOXVILLE: SUMMER OF 1915

We are talking now of summer evenings in Knoxville, Tennessee
in the time that I lived there so successfully disguised as a child.

...It has become that time of evening when people sit on
their porches, rocking gently and talking gently and watching
the street and the standing up into their sphere of possession
of the trees, of birds' hung havens, hangars. People go by;
things go by. A horse, drawing a buggy, breaking his hollow
iron music on the asphalt: a loud auto: a quiet auto: people
in pairs, not in a hurry, scuffling, switching their weight of
aestival body, talking casually, the taste hovering over them
of vanilla, strawberry, pasteboard, and starched milk, the
image upon them of lovers and horsemen, squared with
clowns in hueless amber. A streetcar raising its iron moan;
stopping; belling and starting, stertorous; rousing and raising
again its iron increasing moan and swimming its gold
windows and straw seats on past and past and past, the bleak
spark crackling and cursing above it like a small malignant
spirit set to dog its tracks; the iron whine rises on rising
speed; still risen, faints; halts; the faint stinging bell; rises
again, still fainter; fainting, lifting, lifts, faints foregone:
forgotten. Now is the night one blue dew.

Now is the night one blue dew, my father has drained, he has
coiled the hose.

Low on the length of lawns, a frailing of fire who breathes...

Parents on porches: rock and rock. From damp strings
morning glories hang their ancient faces.

The dry and exalted noise of the locusts from all the air at once enchants my eardrums.

On the rough wet grass of the back yard my father and mother have spread quilts. We all lie there, my mother, my father, my uncle, my aunt, and I too am lying there .... They are not talking much, and the talk is quiet, of nothing in particular, of nothing at all in particular, of nothing at all. The stars are wide and alive, they seem each like a smile of great sweetness, and they seem very near. All my people are larger bodies than mine, ... with voices gentle and meaningless like the voices of sleeping birds. One is an artist, he is living at home. One is a musician, she is living at home. One is my mother who is good to me. One is my father who is good to me. By some chance here they are, all on this earth; and who shall ever tell the sorrow of being on this earth, lying on quilts, on the grass, in a summer evening, among the sounds of the night. May God bless my people, my uncle, my aunt, my mother, my good father, oh, remember them kindly in their time of trouble; and in the hour of their taking away.

After a little I am taken in and put to bed. Sleep, soft smiling, draws me unto her: and those receive me, who quietly treat me, as one familiar and well-beloved in that home: but will not, oh, will not, not now, not ever; but will not ever tell me who I am.

JAMES AGEE
(1909-1955)

LULLABY

Speak to me your darkness
tell me your memory and storms
tell me your darkness and storms
your rivers that are bad and red tell me

sleep little one sleep

a flight of white buildings
the green hills the poppies and one black cat wandering
your darkness your rivers

sleep little one sleep

RUTH KRAUSS

SEARCHLIGHT

At night this child can't sleep.
White light scans the sky,
shines through the window
at the side of her bed.
It's diffuse as it falls
on her pillow, her head,
all spread out.
She's afraid to be held by this light.

Her father calls what she sees a searchlight,
says it's nothing to fear. In a way
she believes him, trusts he's not lying,
can even imagine the machine he describes
a few blocks to the south
where the beam narrows down to a source.

Still, she knows what she knows.
That this circling light is a pathway,
the trail witches ride home.
They've sought her, these witches.
Night after night she lies in their light,
eyes open, unable to sleep.
They've sought her and found her; she's theirs.

She lets light in through her eyes,
lets it swirl in her skull.
This child loves her father
and the small truth he tells her.
But the witches who claim her name more.

JUDITH TANNENBAUM
(1947-   )

Hymn to Selene

O Muses, sing of the far-flying Moon,
you honey-voiced daughters of Zeus, son of Kronos,
who know our songs well.

From heaven streams the light from her head.
It floods the earth, and in its brilliance
all beauty comes forth. The black sky
brightens with her glow. Her rays fill the night
as she bathes in the radiant ocean and dons
garments that shine through a million miles,
as she yokes her burning team and races,
flecked with lightbeams, quarter by quarter
to fullness. Her course run,
she shines her brightest from the height of the heavens
and shows herself as a sign to us mortals.

Zeus once lay with her, and she bore
the maiden Pandea, incomparably beautiful.

Hail white-armed goddess, shining Selene,
you of the glistening flows of gold hair.
I begin my songs with you
and turn them now to the demigods
whom our singers exalt with crystalline voices.

Homeric Hymn
(circa 7th century B.C.E.)
TRANSLATED FROM THE GREEK BY Gregory McNamee

16

There is some kiss we want
with our whole lives,
the touch of Spirit on the body.

Seawater begs the pearl
to break its shell.

And the lily, how passionately
it needs some wild Darling!

At night, I open the window
and ask the moon to come
and press its face against mine.
Breathe into me.

Close the language-door
and open the love window.

The moon won't use the door,
only the window.

RUMI
(1207-1273)
VERSION BY COLEMAN BARKS

On a night
when the moon
shines as brightly as this,
the unspoken thoughts
of even the most discreet heart might be seen.

IZUMI SHIKIBU
(10th-11th century)
TRANSLATED FROM THE JAPANESE BY
JANE HIRSHFIELD WITH MARIKO ARATANI

At times I wonder
   if people in the ancient past
      like myself tonight
Found it difficult to sleep
   due to longing over love.

KAKINOMOTO HITOMARO
(late 7th-early 8th century)
TRANSLATED FROM THE JAPANESE BY HAROLD WRIGHT

You told me it was
because of me
you gazed at the moon.
I've come to see
if this is true.

Izumi Shikibu
(10th-11th century)
TRANSLATED FROM THE JAPANESE BY Willis Barnstone

All night I could not sleep
Because of the moonlight on my bed
I kept on hearing a voice calling:
Out of Nowhere, Nothing answered, "yes."

Tzu Yeh
(3rd-6th century)
TRANSLATED FROM THE CHINESE BY Arthur Waley

Awed by her splendor

Stars near the lovely
moon cover their own
bright faces
               when she
is roundest and lights
earth with her silver

SAPPHO
(7th-6th century B.C.E.)
TRANSLATED FROM THE GREEK BY MARY BARNARD

I cannot say
which is which:
the glowing
plum blossom *is*
the spring night's moon.

IZUMI SHIKIBU
(10th-11th century)
TRANSLATED FROM THE JAPANESE BY
JANE HIRSHFIELD WITH MARIKO ARATANI

Inside water, a waterwheel turns.
A star circulates with the moon.

We live in the night ocean wondering,
What are these lights?

RUMI
(1207-1273)
TRANSLATED FROM THE PERSIAN BY
JOHN MOYNE AND COLEMAN BARKS

QUIET NIGHT THOUGHTS

Before my bed
there is bright moonlight
So that it seems
like frost on the ground:

Lifting my head
I watch the bright moon,
Lowering my head
I dream that I'm home.

LI PO
(701-762)
TRANSLATED FROM THE CHINESE BY ARTHUR COOPER

Oh moon, oh moon!
Who is your mother?
White crescent!
If she frowns at you
bad harvest befalls you.
If she does not—
your mouth will be full.
She gave me charms
for women of any age.
She gave me these two secrets—
but don't ask why.

ELEMA TRIBE, PAPUA, NEW GUINEA
TRANSLATED BY MARI MARASE

THE MOON'S THE NORTH WIND'S COOKY
(WHAT THE LITTLE GIRL SAID)

The Moon's the North Wind's cooky.
He bites it, day by day,
Until there's but a rim of scraps.
That crumble all away.

The South Wind is a baker.
He kneads clouds in his den,
And bakes a crisp new moon *that...greedy*
North...Wind...eats...again!

VACHAL LINDSAY
(1879-1931)

Write about a radish
Too many people write about the moon.

The night is black
The stars are small and high
The clock unwinds its ever-ticking tune
Hills gleam dimly
Distant nighthawks cry.
A radish rises in the waiting sky.

KARLA KUSKIN

Native American Moon Calendars

TLINGIT
goose moon
black bear month
silver salmon month
month before everything hatches
month everything hatches
time of the long days
month when the geese can't fly
month when all kinds of animals prepare their dens
moon child
big moon/formation of ice
month when all creatures go into their dens
ground hog mother's moon

TEWA
ice moon
lizard belly cut moon
month leaves break forth
month when leaves open
tender leaf month/corn planting
dark leaf month
horse month/month of ripeness
wheat cutting month
month when the corn is taken in/syrup is made
harvest month/month of falling leaves
month when all is gathered in
ashes fire

OMAHA
moon in which the snow drifts into the tents of the Hoga
moon in which the geese come home
little frog moon
moon in which nothing happens
moon in which they plant
moon in which the buffalo bulls hunt the cows
moon in which the buffalo bellow
moon in which the elk bellow
moon in which the deer paw the earth
moon in which the deer rut
moon in which the deer shed their antlers
moon in which the little black bears are born

OJIBWA
long moon, spirit moon
moon of the suckers
moon of the crust on the snow
moon of the breaking of snowshoes
moon of the flowers & blooms
moon of strawberries
moon of raspberries
moon of whortle berries
moon of gathering of wild rice
moon of the falling of leaves
moon of freezing
little moon of the spirit

One time I wanted two moons
in the sky.
But I needed someone to look up and see
these two moons
because I wanted to hear him
try and convince the others in the village
of what he saw.
I knew it would be funny.
So, I did it.
I wished another moon up!
There it was, across the sky from the old moon.
Along came a man.
Of course I wished him down that open path.
He looked up in the sky.
He had to see that other moon!
One moon for each of his eyes!
He stood looking up in the sky
a long time.
Then he suspected me, I think.
He looked into the trees
where he thought I might be.
But he could not see me
since I was disguised as the whole night itself!
Sometimes
I wish myself into looking like the whole day,
but this time I was dressed like the whole night.
Then he said,
"There is something strange in the sky tonight."
He said it out loud.

I heard it clearly.
Then he hurried home and I followed him.
He told the others, "You will not believe this,
but there are ONLY two moons
in the sky tonight."
He had a funny look on his face.
Then, all the others began looking into the woods.
Looking for me, no doubt!
"Only two moons, ha! Who can believe you?
We won't fall for that!" they all said to him.
They were trying to send the trick back at me!
This was clear to me!
So, I quickly wished a third moon up there
in the sky.
They looked up and saw three moons.
They had to see them!
Then one man
said out loud, "Ah, there, look up! up there!
There is only one moon!
Well, let's go sleep on this
and in the morning
we will try and figure it out."
They all agreed, and went in their houses
to sleep.
I was left standing there
with three moons shining on me.
There were three.... I was sure of it.

JACOB NIBEGÈNESÁBE
TRANSLATED BY HOWARD A. NORMAN

The thief left it behind—
the moon
at the window.

RYŌKAN
(1758-1831)
TRANSLATED FROM THE JAPANESE BY JOHN STEVENS

Little Nasredin was listening to his teacher reading a passage from the Koran: "God gave brilliance to the sun and radiance to the moon."

"Which is the more useful, the sun or the moon?" asked the teacher.

"The moon," replied Nasredin without a moment's hesitation.

"And why is that?"

"Because the sun only comes out when it's daylight. But the moon lights up the world when it's dark."

The old teacher sighed and deemed it wiser to return to the rules of grammar.

ANONYMOUS

FROM *THE WISHING BONE CYCLE*

All the warm nights
sleep in moonlight

keep letting it
go into you

do this
all your life

do this
you will shine outward
in old age

the moon will think
you are
the moon

SWAMPY CREE
GATHERED AND TRANSLATED BY HOWARD A. NORMAN

The Coming of Darkness

A story told by the Kono people of Sierra Leone says that when God first made the world it never became really dark or cold. The sun shone during the day and at night the moon gave a twilight in which everything could be seen clearly. But one day God called the Bat and gave him a basket to carry to the Moon. In the basket was darkness, but God did not say what the Moon should do with it, though he promised to come and explain later on. The Bat flew off with the basket on his back and set out for the Moon. But on the way he got tired and put down the basket for a rest, and went off to get food. During his absence some animals found the basket by the wayside and started to open it, thinking there was food in it. Just as they were taking the cover off the Bat came back, but darkness had already escaped. Ever since then the Bat sleeps all day long, but in the twilight and dark he begins to fly about everywhere, trying to catch the dark, put it back in the basket, and take it to the Moon according to the command of God. But the Bat never succeeds in catching the darkness, although he chases about in every direction, and before long, day returns and the Bat has to sleep again.

Kono
RETOLD BY GEOFFREY PARRINDER

CYPRESSES

At noon they talk of evening and at evening
Of night, but what they say at night
Is a dark secret.

Somebody long ago called them the Trees
of Death and they have never forgotten.
The name enchants them.

Always an attitude of solitude
to point the paradox of standing
Alone together.

How many years they have been teaching birds
In little schools, by little skills,
How to be shadows.

ROBERT FRANCIS
(1901-1987)

A Clear Midnight

This is thy hour O soul,
   thy free flight into the wordless,
Away from books, away from art,
   the day erased, the lesson done,
Thee fully forth emerging, silent, gazing,
   pondering the themes thou lovest best:
Night, sleep, death and the stars.

WALT WHITMAN
(1819-1892)

Night comes so people can sleep like fish
in black water. Then day.

Some people pick up their tools.
Others become the making itself.

RUMI
(1207-1273)
TRANSLATED FROM THE PERSIAN BY
JOHN MOYNE AND COLEMAN BARKS

NIGHT AND DAY

At night, alone,
the world is a river in me.
Sweet rain falls in the drought.
Leaves grow from lightning-struck trees.

I am across the world from daylight
and know the inside of everything
like the black corn dolls
unearthed in the south.

Near this river
the large female ears of corn listen and open.
Stalks rise up the layers of the world
the way it is said some people emerged
bathed in the black pollen of poppies.

In the darkness, I say,
my face is silent.
Like the corn dolls
my mouth has no more need to smile.

At midnight,
there is an eye in each of my palms.

I said, I have secret powers at night,
dark as the center of poppies,
rich as the rain.

But by morning I am filled up
with some stranger's lies
like those little corn dolls.

Unearthed after a hundred years
they have forgotten everything
in the husk of sunlight
and business
and all they can do is smile.

LINDA HOGAN
(1947-   )

WHAT THE CROW SAID

Though friendly to magic
I am not a man disguised as a crow.

I am night eating the sun.

MICHAEL HANNON
(1939-   )

NIGHT

The cold remote islands
And the blue estuaries
Where what breathes, breathes
The restless wind of the inlets,
And what drinks, drinks
The incoming tide;

Where shell and weed
Wait upon the salt wash of the sea,
And the clear night of stars
Swing their lights westward
To set behind the land;

Where the pulse clinging to the rocks
Renews itself forever;
Where, again on cloudless nights,
The water reflects
The firmament's partial setting;

—O remember
In your narrowing dark hours
That more things move
Than blood in the heart.

LOUISE BOGAN
(1897-1970)

NOCTURN

Night comes, an angel stands
Measuring out the time of stars,
Still are the winds, and still the hours.

It would be peace to lie
Still in the still hours at the angel's feet,
Upon a star hung in a starry sky,
But hearts another measure beat.

Each body, wingless as it lies,
Sends out its butterfly of night
With delicate wings and jewelled eyes.

And some upon day's shores are cast,
And some in darkness lost
In waves beyond the world, where float
Somewhere the islands of the blest.

KATHLEEN RAINE
(1909-   )

Night Sky

There came such clear opening of the night sky,
The deep glass of wonders, the dark mind
In unclouded gaze of the abyss
Opened like the expression of a face.
I looked into that clarity where all things are
End and beginning, and saw
My destiny there: 'So', I said, 'no other
'Was possible ever. This
'Is I. The pattern stands so for ever.'

What am I? Bounded and bounded,
A pattern among the stars, a point in motion
Tracing my way. I am my way: it is I
I travel among the wonders.
Held in that gaze and known
In the eye of the abyss,
'Let it be so', I said,
And my heart laughed with joy
To know the death I must die.

KATHLEEN RAINE
(1909-   )

Owl Woman's Death Song

In the great night my heart will go out,
Toward me the darkness comes rattling.
In the great night my heart will go out.

PAPAGO
TRANSCRIBED BY RUTH M. UNDERHILL

From the Diary of Izumi Shikibu

From darkness
I go onto the road
of darkness.
Moon, shine on me from far
over the mountain edge.

IZUMI SHIKIBU
(10th-11th century)
TRANSLATED FROM THE JAPANESE BY WILLIS BARNSTONE

NIGHT AND SLEEP

At the time of night-prayer, as the sun slides down,
the route the senses walk on closes, the route to the invisible opens.

The angel of sleep then gathers and drives along the spirits;
just as the mountain keeper gathers his sheep on a slope.

And what amazing sights he offers to the descending sheep!
Cities with sparkling streets, hyacinth gardens, emerald pastures!

The spirit sees astounding beings, turtles turned to men,
men turned to angels, when sleep erases the banal.

I think one could say the spirit goes back to its old home;
it no longer remembers where it lives, and loses its fatigue.

It carries around in life so many griefs and loads
and trembles under their weight; they are gone; it is all well.

RUMI
(1207-1273)
TRANSLATED FROM THE PERSIAN
BY ROBERT BLY

Entering Rest

Dear Companion of my day,
You are the Holy Mystery I surrender to
when I close my eyes. I give You myself:
the flaws, the mistakes, the petty
self-congratulations. I give You my dear ones:
my fondest hopes for them, my worries,
and my dark thoughts regarding them.
Take my well-constructed separation from me.
Hold me in Your truth.

This day is already past. I surrender it.
When I think about tomorrow, I surrender it too.
Keep me this night. With You
and in You I can trust not knowing anything.
I can trust incompleteness as a way.
Dark with the darkness, silent with the silence,
help me dare to be that empty one—futureless,
desireless—who breathes Your name even in sleep.

GUNILLA NORRIS
(1939-   )

41

THE STARLIGHT NIGHT

Look at the stars! look, look up at the skies!
O look at all the fire-folk sitting in the air!
The bright boroughs, the circle-citadels there!
Down in dim woods the diamond delves! the elves'-eyes!
The gray lawns cold where gold, where quickgold lies!
Wind-beat whitebeam! airy abeles set on a flare!
Flake-doves sent floating forth at farmyard scare!
Ah, well! it is all a purchase, all is a prize.

Buy then! bid then!—What?—Prayer, patience, alms, vows.
Look, look a May-mess, like on orchard boughs!
Look! March-bloom, like on mealed-with-yellow sallows!
These are indeed the barn; withindoors house
The shocks. This piece-bright paling shuts the spouse
Christ home, Christ and his mother and all his hallows.

GERARD MANLEY HOPKINS
(1844-1889)

HOLY NIGHT

joseph, i afraid of stars,
their brilliant seeing.
so many eyes, such light.
joseph, i cannot still these limbs,
i hands keep moving toward i breasts,
so many stars, so bright.
joseph is wind burning from east
joseph, i shine, oh joseph,   oh
illuminated night.

LUCILLE CLIFTON
(1936-   )

HE WISHES FOR THE CLOTHS OF HEAVEN

Had I the heavens' embroidered cloths,
Enwrought with golden and silver light,
The blue and the dim and the dark cloths;
Of night and light and the half-light.
I would spread the cloths under your feet;
But I, being poor, have only my dreams;
I have spread my dreams under your feet;
Tread softly because you tread on my dreams.

W.B. YEATS
(1865-1939)

Dreams

All night
the dark buds of dreams
open
richly.

In the center
of every petal
is a letter,
and you imagine

if you could only remember
and string them all together
they would spell the answer.
It is a long night,

and not an easy one—
you have so many branches,
and there are diversions—
birds that come and go,

the black fox that lies down
to sleep beneath you,
the moon staring
with her bone-white eye.

Finally, you have spent
all the energy you can
and you drag from the ground
the muddy skirts of your roots

and leap awake
with two or three syllables
like water in your mouth
and a sense

of loss—a memory
not yet of a word,
certainly not yet the answer—
only how it feels

when deep in the tree
all the locks click open,
and the fire surges through the wood,
and the blossoms blossom.

MARY OLIVER
(1935-   )

Purple butterflies
fly at night through my dreams.
Butterflies, tell me,
have you seen in my village
the falling flowers of the wisteria?

YOSANO AKIKO
(1878-1942)
TRANSLATED FROM THE JAPANESE BY
KENNETH REXROTH AND IKUKO ATSUMI

THE DREAM TIME

The dream
Startles me awake
But snakes away
Before I can
Perceive its shape
or purpose.
Poltergeist dream—
It leaves me
Cold and shaking—
Large and empty
As a house.

Once upon
A long ago
There was a boy
Who dreamed he had
Two mothers.
The morning mother
Woke him
With the sun
   Within
   the dream
Fed him
Breakfast
Read him
Grand adventures
Planned his future.

The night mother
Hid her face—
The waning moon
And waited
Patient
As an owl.

The morning mother
Kept him in
A magic garden
Where the bees
And gladioli
Whispered
In his ear
Endearments.
The night mother
Liked to breathe
Upon his neck
Where the jugular
Fluttered, under
Fragile skin
   Within
   the dream.

The morning mother
Brought him
Carefully into
A complex world.
Taught him
Measurement
Responsibility
And taxes.
The night mother
Caught him
In the Dream Time
Taught him so much
Endless fear
That he never was
In later years
Afraid of seeing
All the darkness
In another
Human being.

JACK CEGESTE
(1949-   )

Tonight Everyone in the World
Is Dreaming the Same Dream

Each person lies in their bed, restless,
calling an unknown name.
An angel comes to each and every one
and says: "Choose one hand," its own hands
shimmering behind its back.
"In the right is life, in the left
death, called emptiness." At that moment
sobs are heard all over the earth,
and in the heavenly spheres
a rain of tears.

In the dream I am weeping,
for the angel has no hands,
only wings; and each person gazes
at their own palms, purified and glowing.
One hand holds a spark, the other
a dry coal. Each person
spreads their wings.
The earth is created, and moves us
on our journey
toward remembering.

SUSAN LITWAK
(1954-   )

Is my soul asleep?
Have those beehives that labor
at night stopped? And the water
wheel of thought,
is it dry, the cups empty,
wheeling, carrying only shadows?

No my soul is not asleep.
It is awake, wide awake.
It neither sleeps nor dreams but watches,
its clear eyes open,
far-off things, and listens
at the shores of the great silence.

ANTONIO MACHADO
(1875-1939)
TRANSLATED FROM THE SPANISH BY ROBERT BLY

49

Last night, as I was sleeping,
I dreamt—marvellous error!—
that a spring was breaking
out in my heart.
I said: Along which secret aqueduct,
Oh water, are you coming to me,
water of a new life
that I have never drunk?

Last night, as I was sleeping,
I dreamt—marvellous error!—
that I had a beehive
here inside my heart.
And the golden bees
were making white combs
and sweet honey
from my old failures.

Last night, as I was sleeping,
I dreamt—marvellous error!—
that a fiery sun was giving
light inside my heart.
It was fiery because I felt
warmth as from a hearth,
and sun because it gave light
and brought tears to my eyes.

Last night, as I slept,
I dreamt—marvellous error!—
that it was God I had
here inside my heart.

ANTONIO MACHADO
(1875-1939)
TRANSLATED FROM THE SPANISH BY ROBERT BLY

BUDDHA'S SATORI

For six years sitting alone
   still as a snake
      in a stalk of bamboo
with no family
   but the ice
      on the snow mountain
Last night
   seeing the empty sky
      fly into pieces
         he shook
the morning star awake
   and kept it in his eyes.

MUSŌ SOSEKI
(1275-1351)
TRANSLATED FROM THE JAPANESE BY
W.S. MERWIN AND SŌIKU SHIGEMATSU

NIGHT

The sun never stopped shining and the Cashinahua Indians didn't know the sweetness of rest.

Badly in need of peace, exhausted by so much light, they borrowed night from the mouse.

It got dark, but the mouse's night was hardly long enough for a bite of food and a smoke in front of the fire. The people had just settled down in their hammocks when morning came.

So then they tried out the tapir's night. With the tapir's night they could sleep soundly and they enjoyed the long and much-deserved rest. But when they awoke, so much time had passed that undergrowth from the hills had invaded their lands and destroyed their houses.

After a big search they settled for the night of the armadillo. They borrowed it from him and never gave it back.

Deprived of night, the armadillo sleeps during the daytime.

EDUARDO GALEANO
(1940-   )
TRANSLATED FROM THE SPANISH BY CEDRIC BELFAGE

IN A DARK TIME

In a dark time, the eye begins to see,
I meet my shadow in the deepening shade;
I hear my echo in the echoing wood—
A lord of nature weeping to a tree.
I live between the heron and the wren,
Beasts of the hill and serpents of the den.

What's madness but nobility of soul
At odds with circumstance? The day's on fire!
I know the purity of pure despair,
My shadow pinned against a sweating wall.
That place among the rocks—is it a cave,
Or winding path? The edge is what I have.

A steady stream of correspondences!
A night flowing with birds, a ragged moon,
And in broad day the midnight come again!
A man goes far to find out what he is—
Death of the self in a long, tearless night,
All natural shapes blazing unnatural light.

Dark, dark my light, and darker my desire.
My soul, like some heat-maddened summer fly,
Keeps buzzing at the sill. Which I is I?
A fallen man, I climb out of my fear.
The mind enters itself, and God the mind,
And one is One, freeing in the tearing wind.

THEODORE ROETHKE
(1908-1963)

INSOMNIA

When the bird of sleep
thought to nest
in my eye

it saw the eyelashes
and flew away
for fear of nets.

Abū ʿĀmir ibn al-Hammārah
(12th century)
TRANSLATED BY Cola Franzen
FROM THE SPANISH VERSIONS OF Emilio García Gómez

When I am with you, we stay up all night.
When you're not here, I can't go to sleep.

Praise God for these two insomnias!
And the difference between them.

Rumi
(1207-1273)
TRANSLATED FROM THE PERSIAN BY
John Moyne and Coleman Barks

54

NIGHTS

When I'm without you
I sleep on the couch
or in my bed with books,
pen & paper.

I can't decide
which I love best—
you lying next to me
like an open book
or an open book
lying next to me.

CYN. ZARCO
(1950-   )

Without you
no shadow
and the night

night. To see
heaven one
wants a star.

CID CORMAN
(1924-   )

Lord, Listen

Night draws itself as tight
As a ring around my eyes.
My pulse has changed my blood
To fire, but all is gray

And cold around me. Lord, and in
The living day I dream of death,
Drink it with water, eat it in bread:
On Thy scales all weights fail for my grief.

Lord, listen: in Thy beloved blue
I sang the song of Thy heaven's roof
And in Thy eternal breath did not wake the day.
Before Thee my heart feels shame for its dumb scar.

Where must I end? Lord, in the stars
I looked, and in the moon and the valleys of Thy fruit.
The red wine is already tasteless in the grape
And everywhere, in every core, there's bitterness.

Else Lasker-Schüler
(1869-1945)
Translated from the German by Edouard Roditi

A Love Song

Come to me in the night—we shall sleep closely together.
I am so tired, lonely from being awake.
A strange bird already sang in the dark early morning,
As my dream still wrestled with itself and me.

Flowers open before all the springs
Taking on the color of your eyes...

Come to me in the night on seven-starred shoes
And love shall be wrapped up until late in my tent.
Moons rise from the dusty trunk of heaven.

We shall make love quietly like two rare animals
In the high reeds behind this world.

ELSE LASKER-SCHÜLER
(1869-1945)
TRANSLATED FROM THE GERMAN BY MICHAEL GILLESPIE

Wild nights! Wild nights!
Were I with thee,
Wild nights should be
Our luxury!

Futile the winds
To a heart in port—
Done with the compass,
Done with the chart.

Rowing in Eden!
Ah! the sea!
Might I but moor
Tonight in thee!

EMILY DICKINSON
(1830-1886)

Axis

Through the conduits of blood
my body in your body
                        spring of night
my tongue of sun in your forest
                                    your body a kneading-trough
I red wheat
                Through the conduits of bone
I night I water
                    I forest that moves forward
I tongue
        I body
                    I sun-bone
Through the conduits of night
                                spring of bodies
You night of wheat
                        you forest in the sun
you waiting water
                        you kneading-trough of bones
Through the conduits of sun
                                    my night in your night
my sun in your sun
                        my wheat in your kneading-trough
your forest in my tongue
                            Through the conduits of the body
water in the night
                        your body in my body
Spring of bones
                Spring of suns

Octavio Paz
(1914-   )
translated from the spanish by Eliot Weinberger

This night there are no limits to what may be given.
This is not a night but a marriage,
a couple whispering in bed in unison the same words.
Darkness simply lets down a curtain for that.

RUMI
(1207-1273)
TRANSLATED FROM THE PERSIAN BY
JOHN MOYNE AND COLEMAN BARKS

A night full of talking that hurts,
my worst held-back secrets: Everything
has to do with loving and not loving.
This night will pass.
Then we have work to do.

RUMI
(1207-1273)
TRANSLATED FROM THE PERSIAN BY
JOHN MOYNE AND COLEMAN BARKS

LIST FOR A LONG NIGHT

There is a part of the brain
that knows only faces;
there is a pattern for my hand
   that follows your face only:
      quiet eyes, skin warm and light,
      the upward arching mouth and
      fine hair of stilled phrases.
  All around your moonlike radiance
there is the darkness.

There are confessions, slow tears,
names, stories and our
deep, torn trust…

There is soft rocking yielding sighs
   and touches, brief and restrained.
There are cautious lips meeting
   to bring together the air

  we breathe:
the hours are silent.
     There is the light.

D. PATRICK MILLER
(1953-   )

THE GIFT

This darkness is a rope, not a prison:
hand over hand I haul myself in
to touch your face, to blossom.

My fingers crawl toward heaven
leaving behind whorling shadows;
this darkness is a rope, not a prison.

I follow light through forgotten
canyons and grottos;
I touch your face and know

that even the sun has a mission:
as it climbs, it grows.
This darkness is a rope, not a prison

not a cell from which I hasten.
Freely, hand over hand I follow
to touch your face, to open and open

like a night-blooming jasmine,
or a well widening with echoes:
this darkness is a rope, not a prison,
I touch your face, I blossom.

MAURYA SIMON
(1950-   )

Let us bribe the Moon God
Aloof in high heaven
To make this night as long
As five hundred nights.

PRINCE YUHARA
(8th century)
TRANSLATED FROM THE JAPANESE BY KENNETH REXROTH

Word has it
he's lying
and plans to leave
at daybreak tomorrow—
O Lady Night
engulf us
keep the dawn from us.

NISHPATA
(circa 200 A.D.)
TRANSLATED FROM THE PRAKIT BY ANDREW SCHELLING

FRAGMENTS FROM THE "QASĪDA IN THE RHYME OF NŪN"

Now we are far apart
one from the other
my heart has dried up
but my tears keep falling.

In losing you my days
have turned black.
When I was with you
even my nights were white.

It's as though we never spent
that night together
with no third presence
save our two selves made one,

a night our lucky star
caused even gossips
who would spy on us
to turn away their eyes.

We were two secrets
held by the heart of darkness
until the tongue of dawn
threatened to denounce us.

IBN ZAYDŪN
(1003-1070)
TRANSLATED BY COLA FRANZEN
FROM THE SPANISH VERSIONS OF EMILIO GARCÍA GÓMEZ

On a Dark Night

On a dark night
With love-longings aflame
Oh, unearthly adventure!
I went out without being noticed
My house being now still.

In darkness and secure
By the secret ladder
Oh, unearthly adventure!
In darkness and in ambush
My house being now still.

On that night fore-known
In secret, for no one saw me
Nor did I glance at anything
Without other light and guide
But that in my burning heart.

This guided me
More certainly than noon-day light
To where he awaited me
Whom I have known so well
Where no one else appeared.

Night which itself guides
Night more lovely than the dawn
Night that itself unites
Lover with beloved
Lover in lover transformed.

On my flowering breast
Which I kept for him alone
There he stayed sleeping
And I caressed him.
Fanned by the cedars.

The wind from the turret
Blew through his hair.
With his serene hand
On my wounded neck
And all my senses suspended

I remained myself and I forgot myself
My face rested on my lover:
Everything stopped, and I was outside myself
Leaving me watched over
Forgotten among Mary's lilies.

St. John of the Cross
(1542-1591)
TRANSLATED FROM THE SPANISH BY MARY OPPEN

O God, the stars are shining;
All eyes have closed in sleep:
The kings have locked their doors.
Each lover is alone, in secret, with the one he loves.
And I am here too: alone, hidden from all of them—
With You.

Rābi'a
(717-801)
TRANSLATED BY CHARLES UPTON

67

WHAT IS SLEEP?

Question: What is sleep?
Maharshi: How can you know sleep when you are awake?
The answer is to go to sleep and find out
what it is.

Question: But I cannot know it in this way.
Maharshi: This question must be raised in sleep.

Question: But I cannot raise the question then.
Maharshi: So that is sleep.

SRI RAMANA MAHARSHI
(1879-1950)

WRITING IN THE DARK

It's not difficult.
Anyway, it's necessary.

Wait till morning, and you'll forget.
And who knows if morning will come.

Fumble for the light, and you'll be
stark awake, but the vision
will be fading, slipping
out of reach.

You must have paper at hand,
a felt-tip pen, ballpoints don't always flow,
pencil points tend to break. There's nothing
shameful in that much prudence: those are our tools.

Never mind about crossing your t's, dotting your i's—
but take care not to cover
one word with the next. Practice will reveal
how one hand instinctively comes to the aid of the other
to keep each line
clear of the next.

Keep writing in the dark:
a record of the night, or
words that pulled you from depths of unknowing,
words that flew through your mind, strange birds
crying their urgency with human voices,

or opened
as flowers of a tree that blooms
only once in a lifetime:

words that may have the power
to make the sun rise again.

DENISE LEVERTOV
(1923-   )

Struggling to wake up
Hunting for the sun at night
Exhausted by dawn

DAN ROBERTS
(1948-   )

The Waking

I wake to sleep, and take my waking slow.
I feel my fate in what I cannot fear.
I learn by going where I have to go.

We think by feeling. What is there to know?
I hear my being dance from ear to ear.
I wake to sleep, and take my waking slow.

Of those so close beside me, which are you?
God bless the Ground! I shall walk softly there,
And learn by going where I have to go.

Light takes the Tree, but who can tell us how?
The lowly worm climbs up a winding stair;
I wake to sleep, and take my waking slow.

Great nature has another thing to do
To you and me; so take the lively air,
And, lovely, learn by going where to go.

This shaking keeps me steady. I should know.
What falls away is always. And is near.
I wake to sleep, and take my waking slow.
I learn by going where I have to go.

Theodore Roethke
(1908-1963)

70

Recovering

Dream of the world
speaking to me.

The dream of the dead
acted out in me.

The fathers shouting
across their blue gulf.

A storm in each word,
an incomplete universe.

Lightning in brain,
slow-time recovery.

In the light of October
things emerge clear.

The force of looking
returns to my eyes.

Darkness arrives
splitting the mind open.

Something again
is beginning to be born.

A dance is
dancing me.

I wake in the dark.

Muriel Rukeyser
(1913-1980)

RETURN TO THE WORLD

There's darkness; then there's an opalescent web
on the darkness, lax then taut...

If only it were as easy for you as
for astronauts; for deepsea divers.

Under it all, and undulant, a man
will have to rise from the level

of hundredsucker worms, the globular
comb jellies hanging like japanese lanterns,

stars with fins, stars with teeth,
the tube-eyes, the blind-eyes, cucumbers and moons,

will have to rise then rest
before the final break to air, while blood

remembers its birth barometrics
on land, takes a breath, and accommodates.

Or somebody back from the weightless
spaces beyond direction, beyond the idea of volume

having contents, somebody splashed
down, bound from the capsule at last,

will bide time in re-entry, sorting his nearerness
to other suns' lights out of our light.

At least they have a story to tell,
a rock. I touched one, at the National

Aeronautics and Space Museum. But
you.... There in the final fading

of a dream, before the morning clears
that fog from out of the bramble-thicket

the thinklines in your brain are; or
in illness's last thin sweat.... Already

you don't remember. If only you
could also return to this world

with your knowledge intact:
There is a life around our lives for which we're gills.

The nova and ovary, yes are sisters.
The lungs are small bundles of sky.

ALBERT GOLDBARTH
(1948-   )

NIGHT INTO DAY INTO NIGHT

Lying under the vast star-filled California desert sky, I was enjoying the first dawn of a ten-day vision quest. The first blush of light was peeking over the eastern ridges. I was cuddled up in my sleeping bag on the floor of a very large desert bowl, its rim formed by mountains. To the east they are known as the Last Chance Mountains and are part of the Inyo Range. I never did find out the names of those to the west, but I knew they blocked my view of the Eastern slopes of the great Sierra.

My sleep had been light; often I would open my eyes and check the ever-changing sky. The progress of change was slow; if I slept for half an hour or so between glances I wouldn't miss much of the show. Gradually I could detect an ever-so-subtle light in the eastern sky. The dimmest stars there began to blend in with the newly forming light, and soon only the brightest of planets still shone through the gathering light.

On the western horizon night persisted, with a myriad of stars twinkling from a deep blue sky. Then I noticed the edge of dawn out of the corner of my eye, at about ten o'clock high in the eastern sky. Did I really see it, or was it my imagination? When I looked again, it had disappeared. Oh, it must have been my imagination. I shifted my gaze back and forth from dawn to dusk, from east to west. Ah-ha! There it was again—the edge of dawn. This time I was sure I had seen it. I discovered that if I didn't look at it directly but looked in that direction without focusing my eyes, I definitely could see the edge of dawn. There seemed to be a distinct dividing line between dawn and night, as if some light-filled dome were closing over the sky.

My heart beat faster, as I felt like a voyeur looking in on someone else's intimacies—slightly embarrassed, but unable to look away. I was transfixed. The dome kept covering the sky until at last it reached the western horizon. Now the last vestiges of night were gone. The sun came blasting over the eastern slopes. I knew it would be a hot, dry desert day.

I wanted to observe this same phenomenon in reverse when evening came on, so several nights later I settled into my sleeping bag sometime before dusk. As the light of day began to recede I used my shifting-the-eyes technique, looking for the dome of night. But, oddly, it wasn't coming. In fact, the light seemed to put up a stubborn fight: It would not release so gracefully into night as night had into day. I looked from horizon to horizon, east to west and back again. Surprisingly, there was a ring of light on the entire rim of the horizon. I could not tell where on the horizon the sun had disappeared. No stars were appearing in the east, as I had expected.

Suddenly I saw a star, not on the horizon but straight above me. Now there were two, three—and the brightness of the sky was giving way to a deepening blue. All this was taking place directly overhead. The light, in fortifying its hold on the day, put all of its energy on the horizons and left itself thin at the top of the dome. At last the day could hold out no longer and, opening up to the night sky with a great yawn, it fell back, yielding to the greater presence of night.

At that point I realized something which reversed all my former thinking. Prior to that moment I had always associated night as obscuring the day—a veil of night draping itself over the day, turning everything dark. Now I feel quite the opposite: Night is always there, always surrounding us, like a mother's gentle arms. Day comes and goes for us, but the stars are always there no matter what is going on in our earthly neighborhood. The veil is the light of day. Day veils the true sky.

And now when I look up at the light blue sky of day I feel comforted by the thought that beyond the brightness is the ever-constant, deep darkness of the sky filled with pinpoints of light—I have a sense of profound peace, as I feel myself embraced in the arms of the universe.

JUSTINE TOMS
(1942-   )

DAWN

Watching the moon
at dawn
solitary, mid-sky,
I knew myself completely:
no part left out.

Izumi Shikibu
(10th-11th century)
TRANSLATED FROM THE JAPANESE BY
Jane Hirshfield with Mariko Aratani

In gold sandals
dawn like a thief
fell upon me.

Sappho
(7th-6th century B.C.E.)
TRANSLATED FROM THE GREEK BY Willis Barnstone

At night you come here secretly,
and I want the darkness not to end.
But Night says, *Look, you're holding the sun.*
So you're in charge of daylight!

RUMI
(1207-1273)
TRANSLATED FROM THE PERSIAN BY
JOHN MOYNE AND COLEMAN BARKS

The day creeps in and
the sun slits the darkness
with a golden sword.

JAIVA LARSEN
(1981-   )

Some nights, stay up till dawn,
as the moon sometimes does for the sun.
Be a full bucket pulled up the dark way
of a well, then lifted out into light.

RUMI
(1207-1273)
TRANSLATED FROM THE PERSIAN BY
JOHN MOYNE AND COLEMAN BARKS

THE WHITE STALLION

Pale as the morning star
in the hour of sunrise

he advances proudly,
caparisoned with a saddle of gold.

One who saw him going with me
into battle, envied me and said:

"Who bridled Dawn with the Pleiades?
Who saddled lightning with the half moon"?

ABŪ I-SALT UMAYYAH
(1067-1134)
TRANSLATED BY COLA FRANZEN
FROM THE SPANISH VERSIONS OF EMILIO GARCÍA GÓMEZ

Today, like every other day, we wake up empty
and frightened. Don't open the door to the study
and begin reading. Take down the dulcimer.

Let the beauty we love be what we do.
There are hundreds of ways to kneel and kiss the ground.

RUMI
(1207-1273)
TRANSLATED FROM THE PERSIAN BY
COLEMAN BARKS AND JOHN MOYNE

To Krishna Haunting the Hills

Is it true that black birds infinitely dispersed
wake the dawn,
sing to the god
and welcome the sun?
They sing words of the great god whose bed
is the banyan leaf,
who lives on hills robed with the jungle.

ANDAL
(circa 10th century)
TRANSLATED BY WILLIS BARNSTONE

Shamelessly
orange like a
parrot's beak,
arousing with a lover's
touch the clustered
lotus buds,
I praise this
great wheel the sun—
rising it is an
earring for
the Lady of the East.

VIDYA
(between 650 and 850 A.D.)
TRANSLATED BY ANDREW SCHELLING
FROM THE CLASSICAL SANSKRIT TRADITION

FROM *LONGING FOR DARKNESS*

...I walk early down a muddied fire road on the flank of the mountain. Facing east as I turn toward home in the predawn dark, only the softest light has begun to pearl the horizon.

I am perplexed by the tiny flickers of light going off, like matches being lit and blown out, that I see near the ground. After a moment I realize that these are the glimmer of birds' wings as they flit from bush to bush, hop up and down from the ground. Dawn is still so full of night that I cannot detect the birds until they spread their wings. Then the palest light catches the edge backlit and shows me in the briefest flash illumined, not the bird, but the outspread wing.

CHINA GALLAND
(1943-   )

Hymn to Ra

The truth of what we call our knowing is both light and dark. Men are always dying and waking. The rhythm between we call life. In the night I turn and face myself, the many howling, laughing, pausing in the body of one. Some miracle is about to happen. Some new man unseen wishes to rise and speak. I walk in the dark feeling darkness on my skin. Dawn always begins in the bones. The light stirs me to rise and walk. Lightly I step around the sleeping forms, the bodies of the other selves still dreaming. Nothing has been disturbed except my inner quiet. I am restless, an animal sniffing the wind. The shape of truth is coming.

Death matters, as does life. As it ends it begins again. Knowing that is both my comfort and fear. Perfection is a long road; I shall never see its end—the ribbon of life winds back on itself. At dawn the threads of time unfurl, sunlight streams across the sands. Time reaches in both directions, knotted in the golden orb of the moment. The eye opens, the heart opens, the navel yawns and takes the world in its belly. Beneath him the snake feels the movement of earth. Everything else is sky. This moment is eternity.

This light I call genius, noble being conversant with gods. He goes out, hears the hum of the world, beings of light muttering in every stream. In every rock and tree he hears god songs. Then he returns and tells me what god said. I flow like blood from the god's wounds. I am the god's life made visible. I am how god comes to know himself, his ears, his hands, his eyes. The dreaming selves stir in the dark and follow the distant song of the lyre. We enter grace and beauty. I am Osiris shining.

And at dawn I leave my house and go into the field. Stars fade like memory. Bless the boat of morning that carries us into light. Bless the oars that stir the water causing ripples of consciousness. Bless the northern and southern edges of sky. Bless the eastern and western banks of the river. Bless the oars men in the boat, god's people, his faith, his creation. Bless the face of god above us and the reflection of god on earth below. Bless the veil of clouds that guard his secrets. Bless life stirring below the surface of skin, the discomfort of human weakness and mortality, loss and suffering, the misunderstandings that prick consciousness and prod men toward truth. Bless the goddesses, the wives, the daughters, the mothers, the priestesses. Bless the house of Osiris. Bless this body where the world is gathered. Bless the light in his forehead, in his heart and hands. Bless the sun that shines on every limb.

A creature of light am I.

FROM *AWAKENING OSIRIS*
(circa 1600 B.C.E.)
TRANSLATED FROM THE EGYPTIAN BY NORMANDI ELLIS

The Guiding Light of Eternity

O God, who broughtst me from the rest of last night
Unto the joyous light of this day,
Be Thou bringing me from the new light of this day
Unto the guiding light of eternity.
          Oh! from the new light of this day
     Unto the guiding light of eternity.

Celtic Prayer
Translated from the Gaelic by Alexander Carmichael

Sunrise

Dawn sky, on you I lean my brow
as on a woman's shoulder, sweet.
Sun, like a friend's face turned to me,
you rise from behind the mountain now.

O human beauty of the world,
flesh of the light betrothed to death,
and you, great beating heart of earth
in unimagined depths concealed.

Diego Valeri
(1887-1976)
Translated from the Italian by Michael Palma

August 24, 1961

Is it a new country
In another world of reality
Than Day's?
Or did I live there
Before Day was?

I awoke
To an ordinary morning with gray light
Reflected from the street,
But still remembered
The dark-blue night
Above the tree line,
The open moor in moonlight,
The crest in shadow.
Remembered other dreams
Of the same mountain country:
Twice I stood on its summits
I stayed by its remotest lake,
And followed the river
Towards its source.
The seasons have changed
And the light
And the weather
And the hour.
But it is the same land.
And I begin to know the map
And to get my bearings.

Dag Hammarskjöld
(1905-1961)
Translated from the swedish by Leif Sjöberg and W.H. Auden

Magic Song for Those Who Wish to Live

Day arises
From its sleep,
Day wakes up
With the dawning light.
Also you must arise,
Also you must awake
Together with the day which comes.

THULE ESKIMO

Humming Home Your Shadow

When you get up in the morning, Hoopa Indian children are told, it is important for you to wait until you get your shadow home. When you go to sleep at night, part of you— your shadow—takes off. The part that you've held down all day, the part that you wouldn't let live. When you go to bed, your shadow says, "Now is my chance. I will go out and explore the world that you wouldn't let me touch all day." And off it goes. The shadow has the freedom to go as far away as it wants to, but it has one tie: You have a hum that only *your* shadow knows. And it can never disobey you. So when you get up in the morning, if you remember to hum, your shadow will come back home. Even though it doesn't want to. So when you get up, before you go out, give your own little hum, and your shadow will say, "Oh! I have to go home," and it will come home. And you are never ready for the day until you have taken time to sing the song of your own shadow. Some people say, "I must have gotten up on the wrong side of the bed—I think I'll go back and start over." They've forgotten to hum! Or some people get up at seven, and at ten o'clock they're still saying, "Don't mind me, I'm not all here." They've forgotten to hum! So there is a land of wisdom in remembering to get yourself all here every day. This is taught to the Hoopa tribal children not by saying, "When you get up in the morning you must do this!" but by saying "Hum your song, so your heart and spirit come together."

HOOPA
RETOLD BY SISTER MARIA JOSÉ HOBDAY

Every day is a god, each day is a god, and holiness holds forth in time. I worship each god, I praise each day splintered down, splintered down and wrapped in time like a husk, a husk of many colors spreading, at dawn fast over the mountains split.

I wake in a god. I wake in arms holding my quilt, holding me as best they can inside my quilt.

Someone is kissing me—already. I wake, I cry, "Oh," I rise from the pillow. Why should I open my eyes?

I open my eyes. The god lifts from the water. His head fills the bay. He is Puget Sound, the Pacific; his breast rises from pastures; his fingers are firs; islands slide wet down his shoulders. Islands slip blue from his shoulders and glide over the water, the empty, lighted water like a stage.

Today's god rises, his long eyes flecked in clouds. He flings his arms, spreading colors; he arches, cupping sky in his belly; he vaults, vaulting and spread, holding all and spread on me like skin....

The day is real....

The day is real.... I stand and smooth the quilt.

"Oh," I cry, "Oh!"

ANNIE DILLARD
(1945-   )

AWAKENING GATHA

Waking in the morning
Time smiles in my hand.
This dawn
Lasts all day.

DEENA METZGER
(1936-   )

O God,
Another Night is passing away,
Another Day is rising—
Tell me that I have spent the Night well so I can be at peace,
Or that I have wasted it, so I can mourn for what is lost.
I swear that ever since the first day You brought me back to life,
The day You became my Friend,
I have not slept—
And even if You drive me from your door,
I swear again that we will never be separated—
Because You are alive in my heart.

RĀBI'A
(717-801)
TRANSLATED BY CHARLES UPTON

Take special care to guard your tongue
    before the morning prayer.
Even greeting your fellow, we are told,
    can be harmful at that hour.
A person who wakes up in the morning is
    like a new creation.
Begin your day with unkind words,
    or even trivial matters—
    even though you may later turn to prayer,
    you have not been true to your Creation.
All of your words each day
    are related to one another.
All of them are rooted
    in the first words that you speak.

HASIDIC
TRANSLATED BY ARTHUR GREEN AND BARRY W. HOLTZ

DAY

Will there really be a morning?
Is there such a thing as day?
Could I see it from the mountains,
If I was as tall as they?

Has it feet like water lilies?
Has it feathers like a bird?
Does it come from famous places
Of which I have never heard?

Oh, some scholar! Oh some sailor!
Oh, some wise men from the skies!
Please to tell this little pilgrim
Where the place called morning lies.

EMILY DICKINSON
(1830-1886)

DAY-BLIND

One clap of day and the dream
rushes back
where it came from. For a moment
the ground is still moist with it.
Then day settles. You step onto dry land.

Morning picks out the four
corners, coffeepot, shawl of dust
on a cupboard. Stunned
by brightness, the dream—
where did it go?

All day you grope in a web
of invisible stars. The day sky
soaks them up like dreams. If you could see
in the light,
you'd see what fires

keep spinning, spinning that mesh of threads
around you. They're closer
than you think, hovering,
out there in the blue. You lean
on the warm sill, squinting.

They must be out there in all that dazzle.

CHANA BLOCH
(1939-   )

Morning Poem

Every morning
the world
is created.
Under the orange

sticks of the sun
the heaped
ashes of the night
turn into leaves again

and fasten themselves to the high branches—
and the ponds appear
like black cloth
on which are painted islands

of summer lilies.
If it is your nature
to be happy
you will swim away along the soft trails

for hours, your imagination
alighting everywhere.
And if your spirit
carries within it

the thorn
that is heavier than lead—
if it's all you can do
to keep on trudging—

there is still
somewhere deep within you
a beast shouting that the earth
is exactly what it wanted—

each pond with its blazing lilies
is a prayer heard and answered
lavishly,
every morning,

whether or not
you have ever dared to be happy,
whether or not
you have ever dared to pray.

MARY OLIVER
(1935-   )

SUN DREAMING

When the world was new, the Sun woman made a little baby girl. She was not like other babies, because all her body was shining with light. As she grew older, away in the west in the land beneath the ground, she was still the same. When some other women tried to touch her, her body burned their fingers like fire.

"Why does your daughter carry fire like this?" they asked the Sun woman.

"We are Sun Dreaming, both of us," the girl's mother told them.

"When all the land is dark, my daughter will bring you light. But I, myself, can't come up above the ground. I'm too strong. If I came up and looked at you, up there, I would burn you to ashes."

Still the girl lived with her mother. At first there was darkness everywhere, but when the girl came up into the sky she lit up all the country. "It's true," people said, looking up at her. "She brings light to us all." They were happy to see her there above them.

Every day, she does just the same. When the first birds start to talk, she comes up into the sky and stands there alone to give us light. Then she begins to think of her mother, lonely and waiting for her, and she moves down in the west on her way home. Down she goes, under the ground, to be with her mother, and darkness covers the land. They sleep there together until it is time for the birds to waken again. Then the Sun woman sends her back to us.

"You must go now," she says. "Go and light all the men and women and children, all our relatives up there. It's all right for you to go, but my light is too strong. If I came, I would kill them."

So she takes her daughter on her shoulders, and they hurry across the east. There she lifts her daughter up until she touches the sky.

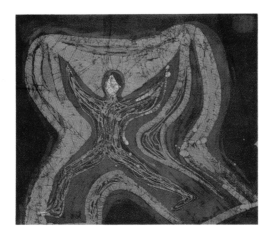

"It's all right now, mother," says the girl. "I'm here. You go back and wait for me." So away she goes under the ground, back to the west.

In the beginning the Sun was a woman like us, but today she is different. Her body looks just like the Rainbow Snake, all bright and shining; and the Sun girl has light and fire all over her body.

They made themselves Dreaming for us, so that we would have light each day to move about, and hunt for our food. If we had no sun and there was night all the time, we couldn't find our way and we couldn't see any animals or plants. We would starve to death.

The moon and the stars give us only a weak light, and the Sun woman is too dangerous for us to see. But the Sun's daughter always looks after us; and every day she makes the country bright, to keep us alive.

AUSTRALIAN
ARRANGED AND TRANSLATED BY CATHERINE H. BERNDT

100

Song for the Sun That Disappeared Behind the Rainclouds

The fire darkens, the wood turns black.
The flame extinguishes, misfortune upon us.
God sets out in search of the sun.
The rainbow sparkles in his hand,
the bow of the divine hunter.
He has heard the lamentations of his children.
He walks along the milky way, he collects the stars.
With quick arms he piles them into a basket
piles them up with quick arms
like a woman who collects lizards
and piles them into her pot, piles them
until the pot overflows with lizards
until the basket overflows with light.

HOTTENTOT
TRANSLATED BY ULLI BEIER

THE SUN

The Sun, dispeller of darkness,
whose eye contemplates all things,
is borne onward by seven shining mares.

His mighty steeds advance
inexorably, like a spider's web,
rendering the night's dark robe.
The rays of the Sun, quivering,
push down beneath the waters
the darkness, like a heavy hide.
How strange the Sun! Untethered,
unsupported, he hangs in space.
Why does he never fall?

What inner power propels him?
Who can observe it? He guards
heaven's vault, the sky's pillar.

RG VEDA
(circa 1400-1200 B.C.E.)
TRANSLATED BY RAIMUNDO PANIKKAR

Shining with the lustre
of moon in autumn
may She, goddess Language
stripping from my
heart the endless woven darkness
cast the nature of all
things into light.

VISHVANATHA
(circa 1350 A.D.)
TRANSLATED BY ANDREW SCHELLING
FROM THE CLASSICAL SANSKRIT TRADITION

No one is ever depressed with you.
Those receiving light give out light.

Secrets cannot be kept
from a confidante.

RUMI
(1207-1273)
TRANSLATED FROM THE PERSIAN BY
JOHN MOYNE AND COLEMAN BARKS

To the Sun

1

Sun, great giver of all that is,
Once more I return from dream to your times and places
As geese wing over London in this morning's dawn
Before the human city invades your immaculate spaces.
Sun, greatest of givers, your speeding rays
Weave again familiar quotidian things, epiphanies
Of trees, leaves, wings, jewelled rain, shining wonders.
Your golden mask covers the unknown
Presence of the awakener of all eyes
On whose blinding darkness none can gaze.
Clouds and hills and gardens and forests and seas,
High-rise buildings, dust and ordure, derelict and broken things
Receive alike from holiest, purest source
Meaning and being, messages each morning brings
To this threshold where I am.
Old, I marvel that I have been, have seen
Your everything and nothing realm, all-giving sun.

2

How address you, greatest of givers,
God, angel, these worlds served once, but no longer
Apollo's chariot or Surya's horses imaged in stone
Of Konarak, glorious metaphor of the advancing power
Of the unwearied sun from the eternal East. My time
Has other symbols, speeding light waves, light-years, rays
Cycling for ever the boundless sphere of space,

Vast emptiness of what is or is not,
Unsolid matter's equivocal seeming—
Science only another grandiose myth we have dreamed,
Ptolemaic or Copernican, or Einstein's paradigm
Less real than those magnificent stone horses
As light triumphs over darkness for yet one more day.
But no myth, as before our eyes you are, or seem!
In your numinous glory I have seen you rise
From beyond the Farne Isles casting your brilliance
Over cold northern seas, or over the seas of Greece,
Have seen your great rim rising from India's ocean.
As you circle the earth birds sing your approach each morning,
New flowers open in wilderness, gardens, waste-places,
All life your retinue, as before all eyes you summon,
Greatest of givers, your heavens outspread
Our earth's vast and minute spaces, to each the whole,
And today I receive yet again from your inexhaustible treasury
Of light, this room, this green garden, my boundless universe.

   3
Ancestral sun, do you remember us,
Children of light, who behold you with living eyes?
Are we as you, are you as we? It seems
As if you look down on us with living face:
Who am I who see your light but the light I see,
Held for a moment in the form I wear, your beams.

I have stood on shores of many seas,
Of lakes and rivers, and always over the waters,
Across those drowning gulphs of fear
Your golden path has come to me
Who am but one among all who depart and return.

Blinding sun, with your corona of flames, your chasms of fire,
Presence, terrible theophany,
Am I in you, are you in me,
Infinite centre of your unbounded realm
Whose multitudes sing Holy, Holy, Holy?
Do you go into the dark, or I?

4

Not that light is holy, but that the holy is the light—
Only by seeing, by being, we know,
Rapt, breath stilled, bliss of the heart.
No microscope nor telescope can discover
The immeasurable: not in the seen but in the seer
Epiphany of the commonplace.
A hyacinth in a glass it was, on my working-table,
Before my eyes opened beyond beauty light's pure living flow.
'It is I,' I knew, 'I am that flower, that light is I,
'Both seer and sight.'
Long ago, but for ever; for none can un-know
Native Paradise in every blade of grass,
Pebble, and particle of dust, immaculate.
'It has been so and will be always,' I knew,

No foulness, violence, ignorance of ours
Can defile that sacred source:
Why should I, one of light's innumerable multitude,
Fear in my unbecoming to be what for ever is?

<small>Kathleen Raine</small>
(1909-   )

At Noontime

When the earth is
bright with flaming
heat falling straight down

the cricket sets
up a high-pitched
singing in his wings

Sappho
(7th-6th century B.C.E.)
TRANSLATED FROM THE GREEK BY MARY BARNARD

Look at a candleflame in bright noon sunlight.
    If you put cotton next to it, the cotton will burn,
        but its light has become completely mixed
            with the sun.

EXCERPT FROM RUMI
(1207-1273)
TRANSLATED FROM THE PERSIAN BY COLEMAN BARKS

MIDDAY PRAYER

God of mercy,
   this midday moment of rest
   is your welcome gift.
   Bless the work we have begun,
   make good its defects
   and let us finish it in a way
   that pleases you.

CHRISTIAN PRAYER

In the quiet of midday
The peony dreams
While low purple clouds
Trail
In the sky.

YOSANO AKIKO
(1878-1942)
TRANSLATED FROM THE JAPANESE BY
SANFORD GOLDSTEIN AND SEISHI SHINODA

Day

The crow, which now dominates the totem of the Haida nation, was the grandson of that great divine chief who made the world.

When the crow kept asking for the moon, which hung from the wall of tree trunks, his grandfather gave it to him. The crow threw it into the sky through the chimney opening and started crying again, wishing for the stars. When he got them he spread them around the moon.

Then he wept and hopped about and screamed until his grandfather gave him the carved wooden box in which he

kept daylight. The great divine chief forbade him to take the box out of the house. He had decided that the world should live in the dark.

The crow played with the box, pretending to be satisfied, but out of the corner of his eye he watched the guards who were watching him.

When they weren't looking, he fled with the box in his claw. The point of the claw split passing through the chimney, and his feathers were burned and stayed black from then on.

The crow arrived at some islands off the northern coast. He heard human voices and asked for food. They wouldn't give him any. He threatened to break the wooden box.

"I've got daylight in here," he warned, "and if it escapes, the sky will never put out its light. No one will be able to sleep, nor to keep secrets, and everybody will know who is people, who is bird, and who is beast of the forest."

They laughed. The crow broke open the box, and light burst forth in the universe.

EDUARDO GALEANO
(1940-   )
TRANSLATED FROM THE SPANISH BY CEDRIC BELFRAGE

Time

For the Maya, time was born and had a name when the sky didn't exist and the earth had not yet awakened.

The days set out from the east and started walking.

The first day produced from its entrails the sky and the earth.

The second day made the stairway for the rain to run down.

The cycles of the sea and the land, and the multitude of things, were the work of the third day.

The fourth day willed the earth and the sky to tilt so that they could meet.

The fifth day decided that everyone had to work.

The first light emanated from the sixth day.

In places where there was nothing, the seventh day put soil; the eighth plunged its hands and feet in the soil.

The ninth day created the nether worlds; the tenth earmarked for them those who had poison in their souls.

Inside the sun, the eleventh day modeled stone and tree.

It was the twelfth that made the wind. Wind blew, and it was called spirit because there was no death in it.

The thirteenth day moistened the earth and kneaded the mud into a body like ours.

Thus it is remembered in Yucatán.

Eduardo Galeano
(1940-   )
Translated from the Spanish by Cedric Belfrage

FROM "LEARNING TO TELL TIME"

One p.m.
    The hour of the dreamer
    the hour that digests
    a sometimes lazy hour that leans on noon
    It is the hour that sometimes wishes it could
    trade places with another hour
    It is the beginning of the downhill hours
    It is the hour of the cat, cleaning, and stretching

Two
    The wonder-what-other-people-are-doing
    hour the hour with a window in it
    the hour which is the child in the
    middle of a big family
    the hour which doesn't always get heard
    the hour that sometimes gets bored

Three
    It is an earnest hour willing
    to try and please
    It is a late August hour
    the hour of anticipation
    It is an hour that has
    some ambition
    It is the hour of
    the goldfish

MARY JO HOMSTAD
(1947-1978)

Oblique Prayer

Not the profound *dark*
night of the soul

and not the austere desert
to scorch the heart at noon,
grip the mind
in teeth of ice at evening

but gray,
a place
without clear outlines,

the air
heavy and thick

the soft ground clogging
my feet if I walk,
sucking them downwards
if I stand.

Have you been here?
Is it

a part of human-ness

to enter
no man's land?

I can remember

        (is it asking you
        that
        makes me remember?)

even here

the blessèd light that caressed the world
before I stumbled into
this place of mere
non-darkness.

DENISE LEVERTOV
(1923-   )

The movement of the sun across our rooms
from window to window, from the morning
to the evening. How many days, how many
seasons, and then years....
Our little girls, then women.
You ever more weary and far, and then
all over, one morning at dawn.
I sit here, to watch in astonishment
time as it moves
through window after window with the old sun.

DIEGO VALERI
(1887-1976)
TRANSLATED FROM THE ITALIAN BY MICHAEL PALMA

There's a certain Slant of light,
   Winter Afternoons—
   That oppresses, like the Heft
   Of Cathedral Tunes—

Heavenly hurt, it gives us—
   We can find no scar,
   But internal difference,
   Where the Meanings, are—

None may teach it—Any—
   'Tis the Seal Despair
   An Imperial affliction
   Sent us of the Air—

When it comes, the Landscape listens—
   Shadows—hold their breath—
   When it goes, 'tis like the Distance
   On the look of Death—

EMILY DICKINSON
(1830-1886)

THE SUN

Look at the beautiful sun
as it rises, it shows one golden eyebrow,
plays miser with the other one,

but we know that soon
it will spread out a radiant veil
over all.

A marvelous mirror
that appears in the East
only to hide again at dusk.

The sky is saddened
when the sun leaves
and puts on mourning robes.

I believe that falling stars
are nothing more
than sky's gem-hard tears.

IBN ABĪ L-HAYTHAM
(d. 1232)
TRANSLATED BY COLA FRANZEN
FROM THE SPANISH VERSIONS OF EMILIO GARCÍA GÓMEZ

VERMEER'S WOMEN

How absent-mindedly they hold the light
that bathes them, the light chilled
against the air before it warms to their skins,
before it enters their calm bodies and
tenderly occupies their faces.
And poised in their faces a completeness
of the self, a sturdy radiance.
How is it the world can be so utterly forgotten
that all the hubbub of horses, vendors,
servant banter, water wheels, and roosters
fades into the stillness of a gesture?
The impasto of colors thickens them,
the damp Delft weather rubs their cheeks
with a soft vermeil rag, and even the details
of their lives—maps, loaves of bread, dogs—
grow lustrous as if such things
gain substance only in the presence
of such women. Spellbound, the world recedes.
And they, with their beauty lost
to themselves by the dailiness of their lives,
pause between centuries,
and by pausing, blaze momentarily
and always.

MAURYA SIMON
(1950-   )

What the Cicada Said

I am Pharaoh
come from the land of the dead.

This is my last incarnation—
one long afternoon outside the window of a fool.

MICHAEL HANNON
(1939-   )

Before the Sun Goes Down

I'll lay my wildflower hand
in your hand's white wicker basket

and bold-tender-shy I'll encircle you
as day and night would encircle
the trees of day and night

and my kisses will live like birds on your shoulder.

ASTRID HJERTENAES ANDERSEN
(1915-1985)
TRANSLATED FROM THE NORWEGIAN BY NADIA CHRISTENSEN

TWILIGHT

CREPUSCULE WITH KATHARINE

Six o'clock. She's closing the store
and I close my eyes. She's the manager here
and since I'm the close friend come to visit
it goes without saying I can steal her chair.
It's staying light later and she lets down the white
shades of rice paper against the dusk. Against the
hour of closing up she lets down her hair, "I didn't
sell one book today, not a one." I don't have to listen
for a kind of cheerfulness-in-the-face-of-adversity.
It's there. It helps the long day settle its hours in me,
like sediment in a cabernet she'd go for in a minute,
like Monk's vintage hesitations on the radio aging
me deliciously. He's playing as if he's missed his cue,
forgotten what comes next, but it's all expert
anticipation. She walks over to the tuner, says
"Let me turn that up for you. For us." Yes, this
is how I'm tuned, by those who know what I want
almost before I do, who offer what I need
without my asking. The dusk deepens in me, opens
my eyes, and her eyes are the color of dusk, deepening,
as she phones her young son, her husband already home
from work. The way Monk's weaving up and down the
keyboard you'd swear he was drunk, or in love or
both. He pauses before each beat, he waits as
you would before the mouth you've never kissed,
the blessed heat of the body you're about to join
your body to. She says the jazz greats
"boil it all down to the basic beautiful."

We listen and don't mention the dutiful calling us
to our separate ways. Monk is playing
the warm dusk and everything within us
and beyond us
goes without saying.

THOMAS CENTOLELLA
(1952-   )

The fountain and the four
acacias in flower
in the garden.
The sun doesn't burn now.
Wonderful dusk!
Nightingale, sing.
The same hour has come
inside my body.

ANTONIO MACHADO
(1875-1939)
TRANSLATED FROM THE SPANISH BY ROBERT BLY

XI.25   We are not great connoisseurs of the two twilights. We miss the dawning, excusably enough, by sleeping through it, and are as much strangers to the shadowless welling-up of day as to the hesitant return of consciousness in our slowly waking selves. But our obliviousness to evening twilight is less understandable. Why do we almost daily ignore a spectacle (and I do not mean sunset but rather the hour, more or less, afterward) that has a thousand tonalities, that alters and extends reality, that offers, more beautifully than anything man-made, a visual metaphor of peace? To say that it catches us at busy or tired moments won't do; for in temperate latitudes it varies by hours from solstice to solstice. Instead I suspect that we shun evening twilight because it offers two things which, as insecurely rational beings, we would rather not appreciate; the vision of irrevocable cosmic change (indeed, change into darkness), and a sense of deep ambiguity—of objects seeming to be more, less, other than we think them to be. We are noontime and midnight people, and such devoted camp-followers of certainty that we cannot endure seeing it mocked and undermined by nature. There is a brief period of twilight of which I am especially fond, little more than a moment, when I see what seems to be color without light, followed by another brief period of light without color.

The earlier period, like a dawn of night, calls up such sights as at all other times are hidden, wistful half-formless presences neither of day nor night, that draw up with them similar presences in the mind.

ROBERT GRUDIN
(1938-   )

Does sunset sometimes look like the sun's coming up?
Do you know what a faithful love is like?
You're crying. You say you've burned yourself.
But can you think of anyone who's not
hazy with smoke?

RUMI
(1207-1273)
TRANSLATED FROM THE PERSIAN BY
JOHN MOYNE AND COLEMAN BARKS

What is it
about this twilight hour?
Even the sound
of a barely perceptible breeze
pierces the heart.

IZUMI SHIKIBU
(10th-11th century)
TRANSLATED FROM THE JAPANESE BY
JANE HIRSHFIELD WITH MARIKO ARATANI

Evening says to night:
"Are you always this beautiful under your clothes?"
Night says to the moon:
"All day I dreamed of you but I couldn't bring myself to call."
The moon says to sleep:
"There are doorways in the dark."
Sleep says to dawn:
"As if forward were the only direction!"

Dawn says to early morning sun:
"Sing sung sun"
Morning says to noon:
"Trees also do research."
Noon says to early afternoon:
"Builders and dreamers need to listen to each other."
Early afternoon says to late afternoon:
"I am becoming possible."
Late afternoon says to the setting sun:
"Tell me about the texture of fire."
The sunset says to the twilight:
"In a circle there is no beginning or end."

Twilight to the first star says:
"Thank you for your light."
First star to evening:
"Thank you for your dark."

J. RUTH GENDLER
(1954-   )

And Suddenly It Is Evening

Everyone stands alone at the heart of this earth
Stunned by a ray of sunlight
and suddenly it is evening.

SALVATORE QUASIMODO
(1901-1968)
TRANSLATED FROM THE ITALIAN BY J. RUTH GENDLER

Responsive Reading

Light and darkness, night and day.
We marvel at the mystery of the stars.
Moon and sky, sand and sea.
We marvel at the mystery of the sun.
Twilight, high noon, dusk and dawn.
Though we are mortal, we are Creation's crown.
Flesh and bone, steel and stone.
We dwell in fragile, temporary shelters.
Grant steadfast love, compassion, grace.
Sustain us, Lord; our origin is dust.
Splendor, mercy, majesty, love endure.
We are but little lower than the angels.
Resplendent skies, sunset, sunrise.
The grandeur of Creation lifts our lives.
Evening darkness, morning dawn.
Renew our lives as You renew all time.

FROM *SIDDUR SIM SHALOM*
TRANSLATED FROM THE HEBREW BY RABBI JULES HARLOW

The woman who is separated from her lover
spins at the spinning wheel.

The Bagdad of the body rises with its towers and gates.
Inside it the palace of intelligence has been built.

The wheel of ecstatic love turns around in the sky,
and the spinning seat is made of the sapphires of
work and study.

This woman weaves threads that are subtle,
and the intensity of her praise makes them fine!

Kabir says: I am that woman.
I am weaving the linen of night and day.

When my Lover comes and I feel his feet,
the gift I will have for him is tears.

KABĪR
(1440-1518)
TRANSLATED BY ROBERT BLY

POEM

The spirit
  likes to dress up like this:
    ten fingers,
      ten toes,

shoulders, and all the rest
  at night
    in the black branches,
    in the morning

in the blue branches
  of the world.
    It could float, of course,
      but would rather

plumb rough matter.
  Airy and shapeless thing,
    it needs
      the metaphor of the body,

lime and appetite,
  the oceanic fluids;
    it needs the body's world
      instinct

and imagination
  and the dark hug of time,
    sweetness
      and tangibility,

to be understood,
  to be more than pure light
    that burns
      where no one is—

so it enters us—
  in the morning
    shines from brute comfort
      like a stitch of lightning;

and at night
  lights up the deep and wondrous
    drownings of the body
      like a star.

MARY OLIVER
(1935-   )

Personal Acknowledgments

One thousand thanks to Marian O'Brien, graphic designer and creative collaborator, for her vision, perseverance, clarity, and friendship. Thanks also to Rick Kot, Sheila Gillooly, Brad Bunnin, Judy Harbaugh, and to Keith and Quinn Whitaker for making this project possible.

Special thanks to Heidi Gundlach for her careful and enthusiastic reading of the manuscript and her listening which enabled me to have more faith in my own process. Lorraine Andersen generously shared her familiarity with permissions and her understanding of the joys and frustrations of making an anthology. Hallie Inglehart Austen graciously alerted me to the tasks of permissions. For listening to me read these pieces, compare translations, sort, glean, organize, and agonize as I cut material I am indebted to Karen Farhner, Valerie Geller, Jeremy Griffith, Judith Nasaw, Shana Penn. Thanks to Laurence Ostrow for his appreciation of changing light, especially at dawn and sunset, to Jack Foley for telling me the root meaning of anthology as a "gathering of flowers," to Mark Goldstein for bringing so many kinds of sound to light. For loaning books and suggesting sources, I am grateful to Anita Barrows, John Boe, Kathy Evans, Dorothy Fadiman, Sylvia Gaddas, Sue Gartley, Catherine Girardeaux, Mary Elizabeth McGann, Gabriele Rico, Georgia Schwimmer, Jonathan Seidel. Miscellaneous and many thanks to the Gendler family. Many, many people contributed to this project, sharing their knowledge of various traditions. Though it would be impossible to thank them all individually, I am deeply grateful for their suggestions and directions.

Finally, it is with immense appreciation I acknowledge all my art teachers, artist friends, and walking companions who traveling with me have reminded me to look and keep looking at what I am seeing.

ACKNOWLEDGMENTS OF SOURCES

Every effort has been made to trace copyright. If any omissions or errors have been made, please let us know and we will remedy future editions. We gratefully acknowledge the following permissions.

James Agee, "Knoxville: Summer of 1915," from *A Death in the Family*. Copyright © 1957 by The James Agee Trust, copyright renewed © 1985 by Mia Agee. Reprinted by permission of Grosset & Dunlap, Inc.

Abu 'Amir ibn al-Hammarah, "Insomnia"; Abu l-Salt Umayyah, "The White Stallion"; Ibn Abi l-Haytham, "The Sun"; Ibn Zaydun, Fragments from the "Qasida in the Rhyme of Nun"; Muhammad ibn Ghalib al-Rusafi, "Serene Evening," translated by Cola Franzen in *Poems of Arab Andalusia*. Copyright © 1989 by Cola Franzen. Reprinted by permission of City Lights Books.

Yosano Akiko, "Purple butterflies," from Kenneth Rexroth, *Women Poets of Japan*, translated by Kenneth Rexroth and Ikuko Atsumi. Copyright © 1977 by Kenneth Rexroth and Ikuko Atsumi. Reprinted by permission of New Directions. "In the quiet of midday," translated by Sanford Goldstein and Seishi Shinoda in *Tangled Hair*. Copyright © 1987 by Charles E. Tuttle Company. Used by permission of Charles E. Tuttle Company.

Anna Akmatova, "A land not mine," translated by Jane Kenyon. This translation first appeared in *News from the Universe*, edited by Robert Bly. Reprinted by permission of Jane Kenyon.

Andal, "To Krishna Haunting the Hills," translated by Willis Barnstone in *A Book of Women Poets from Antiquity to Now* by Aliki and Willis Barnstone. Copyright © 1980 by Schocken Books Inc. Reprinted by permission of Schocken Books, published by Pantheon Books, a division of Random House, Inc.

Astrid Hjertenaes Anderson, "Before the Sun Goes Down," reprinted by permission of H. Aschehoug and Co., Oslo, Norway.

Basho excerpt translated by Sam Hamill in *Basho's Ghost*, Broken Moon Press. Copyright © 1989 by Sam Hamill. Used by permission of Sam Hamill.

Chana Bloch, "Day-Blind," from *The Past Keeps Changing*. Copyright © 1992 by Chana Bloch. Published by Sheep Meadow Press. Used by permission of the author.

Louise Bogan, "Night," from *The Blue Estuaries* by Louise Bogan. Copyright © 1968 by Louise Bogan. Reprinted by permission of Farrar, Straus & Giroux, Inc.

Joseph Bruhac, "How Mink Stole Time," reprinted by permission of Joseph Bruhac.

Jack Cegeste, "The Dream Time," from *In Relationship to Light*. Used by permission of the author.

Thomas Centolella, "Crepuscule with Katharine," from *Terra Firma*, Copper Canyon Press. Copyright © 1990 by Thomas Centolella. Reprinted by permission of the author.

lucille clifton, "holy night," from *good woman: poems and a memoir 1969–1980*, BOA Editions. Copyright © 1987 by lucille clifton. Reprinted by permission of Curtis Brown, Ltd.

Cid Corman, "Without You." Copyright © 1991 by Cid Corman. Reprinted by permission of the author.

Annie Dillard, excerpt from *Holy the Firm*. Copyright © 1977 by Annie Dillard. Reprinted by permission of Harper & Row.

Elema Tribe, "Oh moon, oh moon!," translated by Mari Marase from *Words of Paradise: Poetry of Papua New Guinea*, edited by Georgina and Ulli Beier. Copyright © 1973 by Georgina and Ulli Beier. Used by permission of Unicorn Press.

Robert Francis, "Cypresses," from *The Orb Weaver*. Copyright © 1960 by Robert Francis. Reprinted by permission of Wesleyan University Press and University Press of New England.

Eduardo Galeano, "Day," "Night," and "Time," from *Memories of Fire: Genesis*, translated by Cedric Belfrage. Copyright © 1985 by Cedric Belfrage. Reprinted by permission of Pantheon Books, a division of Random House, Inc.

China Galland, excerpt from *Longing for Darkness*. Copyright © 1990 by China Galland. Reprinted by permission of Viking Penguin.

J. Ruth Gendler, "Evening says to night." Copyright © 1990 by J. Ruth Gendler.

Jacob Glatstein, "Praying the Sunset Prayer," translated by Ruth Whitman from *The Selected Poems of Jacob Glatstein*. Copyright © 1972 by Ruth Whitman. Reprinted by permission of October House, Publishers.

"God of Mercy" from *The Liturgy of the Hours*, English translation. Copyright © 1974 by International Committee on English in the Liturgy, Inc.

Albert Goldbarth, "Return to the World," from *Original Light: New & Selected Poems 1973–1983*. Copyright © 1983 by Albert Goldbarth. Reprinted by permission of Ontario Review Press.

Robert Grudin, From *Time and the Art of Living*. Copyright © 1982 by Robert Grudin. Used by permission of Harper & Row.

Dag Hammarskjold, "You wake from dreams of doom" and "August 24, 1961," translated by Leif Sjoberg, W.H. Auden, from *Markings*. Translation copyright © 1964 by Alfred A. Knopf, Inc., and Faber & Faber Ltd. Reprinted by permission of Alfred A. Knopf, Inc.

Michael Hannon, "What the Crow Said," "What the Rose Said," and "What the Cicada Said," from *Venerations & Fables*, Turkey Press. Copyright © 1982 by Michael Hannon. Used by permission of Michael Hannon.

Kakinomoto Hitomaro, "At times I wonder," translated by Harold Wright from *Ten Thousand Leaves: Love Poems from the Manyoshu*. Copyright © 1979 by Harold Wright. Used by permission of Overlook Press.

Linda Hogan, "Night and Day," from *Seeing through the Sun*. Copyright © 1985 by Linda Hogan. Reprinted by permission of University of Massachusetts Press.

Hottentot "Song for the Sun That Disappeared Behind the Rainclouds," from *African Poetry: An Anthology of Traditional African Poems*, compiled and edited by Ulli Beier. Copyright © 1966. Used by permission of Cambridge University Press.

Ping Hsin, "The orphan boat of my heart," translated by Kenneth Rexroth and Ling Chung in *Women Poets of China*. Copyright © 1972 by Kenneth Rexroth and Ling Chung. Reprinted by permission of New Directions.

"Hymn to Ra," from *Awakening Osiris: The Egyptian Book of the Dead*, translated by Normandi Ellis. Copyright © 1988 by Normandi Ellis. Reprinted by permission of Phanes Press.

"Hymn to Selene," translated by Gregory McNamee. Copyright © 1991 by Gregory McNamee.

Kabir, "The woman who is separated…," translated by Robert Bly from *The Kabir Book*. Copyright © 1971 by the Seventies Press and Robert Bly. Reprinted by permission of Beacon Press.

Karla Kuskin, "Write about a radish," from *Near the Window Tree*. Copyright © 1975 by Karla Kuskin. Used by permission of Harper & Row.

Jaiva Larsen, "The day creeps in…," reprinted from *Images*, Moving Parts Press. Used by permission of Annise Jacoby and Jaiva Larsen.

Else Lasker-Schuler, "Lord, Listen…," translated by Edouard Roditi in *Thrice Chosen*. English translation copyright © 1981 by Edouard Roditi. Reprinted by permission of Black Sparrow Press. "A Love Song," translated by Michael Gillespie in *A Book of Women Poets from Antiquity to Now* by Aliki and Willis Barnstone.

Denise Levertov, "Oblique Prayer," from *Oblique Prayers*. Copyright © 1984 by Denise Levertov, and "Writing in the Dark," from *Candles in Babylon*. Copyright © 1982 by Denise Levertov. Used by permission of New Directions.

Li Po, "Quiet Night Thoughts," translated by Arthur Cooper from *Li Po and Tu Fu*. Copyright © 1973 by Arthur Cooper. Used by permission of Penguin Classics.

Susan Litwak,"Tonight Everyone in the World Is Dreaming the Same Dream." Copyright © 1980, 1991 by Susan Litwak. Used by permission of the author.

Antonio Machado, "The fountain and the four/acacias in flower," "Last night, as I was sleeping," and "Is my soul asleep?," translated by Robert Bly in *Times Alone*, Wesleyan University Press. Translation copyright © 1983 by Robert Bly. Reprinted by permission of Robert Bly.

"Magic Song for Those Who Wish to Live," Thule Eskimo, translated by Knud Rasmussen in *I Breathe a New Song*, edited by Richard Lewis, Simon & Schuster. Used by permission of Richard Lewis.

Sri Ramana Maharshi, "What Is Sleep?," in *Talks with Sri Ramana Maharshi*, Tiruvannamalai, S. India, 1958. Used by permission of the publisher.

Deena Metzger, "Awakening Gatha," from *Looking for the Faces of God*. Copyright © 1989 by Deena Metzger. Reprinted by permission of Parallax Press.

D. Patrick Miller, "Early Darkness" and "List for a Long Night." Copyright © 1978 for "List for a Long Night" and copyright © 1987 for "Early Darkness" by D. Patrick Miller. Used by permission of the author.

Pablo Neruda, "If each day falls/inside each night," translated by William O'Daly, in *The Sea and the Bells*. Translation copyright © 1988 by William O'Daly. Used by permission of Copper Canyon Press.

Nishpata, "Word has it/he's lying"; Vidya, "Shamelessly/orange like a"; Vishvanatha, "Shining with the lustre," translated by Andrew Schelling in *Dropping the Bow: Poems from Ancient India*, Broken Moon Press, 1991. Used by permission of Andrew Schelling.

Howard Norman, translator, "All the warm nights/sleep in moonlight" and "One time I wanted two moons/in the sky," by Jacob Nibegenesabe in *The Wishing Bone Cycle*. Copyright © 1972 by Howard Norman. Reprinted by permission of Ross-Erikson Publishing.

Gunilla Norris, "Entering Rest," in *Being Home: A Book of Meditations*. Text copyright © 1991 by Gunilla Norris. Reprinted by permission of Bell Tower, an imprint of Harmony Books, a division of Crown Publishers, Inc.

Mary Oliver, "Morning Poem," "Poem," and "Dreams," from *Dream Work* by Mary Oliver. Copyright © 1986 by Mary Oliver. Used by permission of Atlantic Monthly Press.

"Owl Woman's Death Song," transcribed by Ruth M. Underhill from *Papago Indian Religions*. Reprinted by permission of Columbia University Press.

Geoffrey Parrinder, "The Coming of Darkness," in *African Mythology*. Copyright © 1967, 1982 by Geoffrey Parrinder. Used by permission of Peter Bedrick Books.

Octavio Paz, "Axis," translated by Eliot Weinberger, from *The Collected Poems of Octavio Paz, 1957–1987*. Copyright © 1986 by Octavio Paz and Eliot Weinberger. Reprinted by permission of New Directions.

Raimundo Pannikar, "The Dispeller of Darkness," from *The Vedic Experience*. Copyright © 1976. Reprinted by permission of University of California Press.

Rabi'a, "O God,/Another Night is passing away," and "O God, the stars are shining," translated by Charles Upton in *Doorkeeper of the Heart: Versions of Rabi'a*. Copyright © 1988 by Charles Upton. Reprinted by permission of Threshold Books.

Kathleen Raine, "To The Sun," "Nocturn," and "Night Sky," from *Selected Poems*. Copyright © 1988 by Kathleen Raine. Reprinted by permission of Lindisfarne Press.

Rainer Maria Rilke, "Sunset," from *Selected Poems of Rainer Maria Rilke*. English translation copyright © 1981 by Robert Bly. Reprinted by permission of Harper & Row.

Dan Roberts, "Struggling to wake up," from *Hunting for the Sun at Night*. Copyright © 1988 by Dan Roberts. Reprinted by permission of the author.

Theodore Roethke, "In a Dark Time," Copyright © 1969 by Beatrice Roethke, Administratrix of the Estate of Theodore Roethke. "The Waking," from *The Collected Poems of Theodore Roethke*. Copyright © 1948 by Theodore Roethke. Used by permission of Doubleday, a division of Bantam Doubleday Dell Publishing Group, Inc.

Muriel Rukeyser, "Recovering." Copyright © by Muriel Rukeyser. Used by permission of William L. Rukeyser.

Rumi, translated by John Moyne and Coleman Barks, "When I am with you, we stay up all night," "Today, like every other day, we wake up empty," and "Does sunset sometimes look like the sun's coming up?," in *Open Secret*. Copyright © 1984. Used by permission of Threshold Books. "Night goes back to where it was," "This night there are no limits to what may be given," "Night comes so people can sleep like fish," "A night full of talking that hurts," "Inside water, a waterwheel turns," "No one is ever depressed with you," "Some nights, stay up till dawn," and "At night you come here secretly," translated by John Moyne and Coleman Barks in *Unseen Rain*. Copyright © 1986. Used by permission of Threshold Press. "Night and Sleep," translated by Robert Bly in *Night and Sleep*. Copyright © 1981 by Yellow Moon Press. Used by permission of Robert Bly. "There is some kiss we want," version by Coleman Barks in *Like This: 43 Odes*, Maypop. Copyright © 1990 by Coleman Barks. Used by permission of Coleman Barks.

Ryokan, "The thief left it behind," from *One Robe, One Bowl: The Zen Poetry of Ryokan*, translated by John Stevens. Reprinted by permission of Weatherhill.

Sappho, "In gold sandals," translated by Willis Barnstone in *Sappho and the Greek Lyric Poets* by Willis Barnstone. Copyright © 1962, 1967, 1988 by Willis Barnstone. Reprinted by permission of Schocken Books Inc., published by Pantheon Books, a division of Random House, Inc. "At Noontime" and "Awed by her splendor," translated by Mary Barnard in *Sappho: A New Translation*. Copyright © 1958 by the Regents of the University of California. Reprinted by permission of the University of California Press.

Izumi Shikibu, "Watching the moon/at dawn," "On a night/when the moon," "What is it/about this twilight hour," and "I cannot say/which is which" translated by Jane Hirshfield with Mariko Aratani in *The Ink Dark Moon*. Copyright © 1990 by Jane Hirshfield and Mariko Aratani. Reprinted by permission of Vintage Books, a division of Random House. "You told me it was/because of me," "From darkness/I go onto the road," and "Someone else/looked at the sky," translated by Willis Barnstone in *A Book of Women Poets from Antiquity to Now* by Aliki and Willis Barnstone. Copyright © 1980 by Schocken Books Inc. Reprinted by permission of Schocken Books, published by Pantheon Books, a division of Random House, Inc.

Siddur sim Shalom, "Evening Prayer," and "Responsive Reading," from *Siddur sim Shalom*, edited, with translations, by Rabbi Jules Harlow. Published by the Rabbinical Assembly and the United Synagogue of America. Copyright © 1985 by the Rabbinical Assembly. Reprinted by permission.